DRIVING
BRITAIN

NORFOLK

Patricia G. Dalton

Little Hills Press

Photographs by author
Illustrations by Victoria Schmorl
Cover by NB Design
Maps by MAPgraphics
Printed in Hong Kong by Magnum International Printing Co Ltd

ISBN 1 86315 095 1

Little Hills Press
Regent House
37-43 Alexander Street
Crows Nest NSW 2065
Australia

Front Cover: Horsey Mill, Norfolk Broad.
Back Cover: The Gatehouse entrance, Heydon Hall.

All distances mentioned in this book are in miles, to correspond with local signposts.
1 mile = 1.6km.

CONTENTS

ACKNOWLEDGEMENTS

In England

Lindsay Want of the East Anglia Tourist Board, Hadleigh, Suffolk, for supplying wonderful information.

Sally and Geoff Marshall, The Old Rectory, Salle. Thank you both for being so very kind and for making me so welcome during my stay in your delightful cottage.

Nick Shipsey, Blakes Holidays Afloat in Wroxham, Norfolk. Thank you Nick, for allowing me the privilege of being associated with your company and facilities. Hopefully I will be able to do some cruising on the Broads next time.

Budget Rent-A-Car, who supplied a wonderful Ford Mondeo, and for the most efficient service and invaluable information received. A special thanks to the team at Dulwich.

In Australia

Catherine Thomas. Without your valued friendship, support, and the typing of some of my research, this book would not look as well presented as it does.

Dr John Farmer. Thank you John for all the support and kindness shown in getting me through some difficult times and for always being there when I needed you.

Dr Peter Roberts. Peter (my wonderful chiropractor) without you this series of books would not have been possible. Thank you for all the tireless hours you put into getting me back on my feet again.

British Tourist Authority in Sydney. Thank you, *Donna Wales*, for your assistance in providing a wealth of information for me.

Lastly, to my sons *Anthony* and *Alastair*, thank you for the love and support you have given me all these years. The East Anglian series of books are dedicated to you both.

A special thanks to my wonderful daughter-in-law *Jennifer* for all the time spent deciphering tapes and typing notes.

INTRODUCTION

East Anglia is made up of the delightful counties of: Suffolk, Norfolk, Essex and Cambridgeshire. Bedfordshire is sometimes included with East Anglia, depending on which maps and books you read.

When I decided to go on holiday to England I bought all the usual travel guides. I don't know how other travellers managed to tour the villages and countryside, but I found it extremely difficult trying to plan a holiday and see places when the information available was in alphabetical order.

The following tours are set out in such a way that travellers can start in a large county town and then travel through the countryside using lanes, smaller arterial roads and by-ways to discover the real country villages.

The **Index of Sights** shows places of interest, which are numbered to correspond with the appropriate tour. Sports and recreation venues are also listed, as are hospitals, police stations and information centres. Included are market days and early closing days, as it is very frustrating to arrive in a town to find that shops are closed or that the town centre is a hive of activity and parking is a problem.

I hope you enjoy the tours you take. The scenery throughout the year is forever changing and it is well worth visiting the out of the way villages with their special place of interest.

The pubs are truly delightful and meals are very reasonable in all those mentioned in this book. Accommodation is of course very plentiful with Bed & Breakfast homes being very popular. If you are going to tour a particular county it may be more suitable and economical to rent a self catering cottage or apartment. The listed accommodation has been visited or stayed in, and are highly recommended at the time of printing.

SCOTLAND

North Sea

Irish Sea

ENGLAND

Norfolk

WALES

London

NORTH

| 0 | miles | 90 |

| 0 | kilometres | 150 |

SUMMARY OF TOURS

Tour 1 - Norwich

Tour 2 - Norwich country tour
Horsford, Aylsham, Blickling, Saxthorpe, Briston, Melton Constable, Hindolveston, Thurning, Wood Dalling, Salle, Heydon, Cawston, Swanington, Norwich

Tour 3 - Norwich to Great Yarmouth
North Burlingham, Acle, Great Yarmouth, Caister-on-Sea, Ormesby St Margaret, Ormesby St Michael, Rollesby, Bastwick, Thurne, Acle, Norwich

Tour 4 - Norwich to the Broads
Sprowston, Wroxham, Hoveton, Horning, Ludham, Potter Heigham, Bastwick, Martham, Winterton-on-Sea, Somerton, Horsey, Waxham, Sea Palling, Hickling, Sutton, Stalham, Coltishall, Norwich

Tour 5 - Norwich to Cromer
Marsham, Erpingham with Calthorpe, Aldborough, Thurgarton, Hanworth, Roughton, Crossdale Street, Felbrigg, Cromer, West Runton, Sheringham, Upper Sheringham, Bodham, High Kelling, Holt, Baconsthorpe, Plumstead, Little Barningham, Itteringham, Horsford, Norwich

Tour 6 - Norwich to North Walsham
Hevingham, Marsham, Tuttington, Banningham, Felmingham, Antingham, Thorpe Market, Northrepps, Overstrand, Sidestrand, Trimingham, Mundesley, Paston, Bacton, Keswick, Walcott, Happisburgh, Whimpwell Green, Lessingham, East Ruston, Honing, Worstead, North Walsham, Lamas, Norwich

Tour 7 - Norwich to Reedham, Broads & Burgh Castle
Thurton, Loddon, Reedham, Freethorpe, Halvergate, Stracey Arms, Burgh Castle, Belton, Fritton, St Olaves, Haddiscoe, Toft Monks, Maypole Green, Raveningham, Hales, Kirby Cane, Kirby Row, Ellingham, Broome, Ditchingham, Kirstead Green, Brooke, Poringland, Norwich

Tour 8 - Norwich to Scole
Caister St Edmund, Stoke Holy Cross, Saxlingham, Nethergate,

Hempnall, Fritton, Morningthorpe, Pulham St Mary, Pulham Market, Dickleborough, Scole, Gissing, Long Stratton, Tasburgh, Newton Flotman, Swainsthorpe, Norwich

Tour 9 - Norwich to Fakenham & Gressenhall
Taverham, Attlebridge, Alderford, Great Witchingham, Reepham, Bawdeswell, Foxley, Bintree, Twyford, Guist, Fakenham, Brisley, East Bilney, Gressenhall, Beetley, North Elmham, Worthing, Swanton Morley, Norwich

Tour 10 - Norwich to Diss
Swardeston, Bracon Ash, Tacolneston, Forncett End, New Buckenham, Banham, Winfarthing, Shelfhanger, Diss, Roydon, Bressingham, North & South Lopham, Kenninghall, Old Buckenham, Puddledock, Attleborough, Norwich

Tour 11 - Norwich to Wymondham & Thetford
Wymondham, Larling, East Harling, Garboldisham, Blo Norton, Thelnathan, Thetford, Wretham, Breckles, Watton, Shipdham, East Dereham, Norwich

Tour 12 - Norwich to Wells next the Sea
Horsford, Saxthorpe, Edgefield, Letheringsett, Glandford, Wiveton, Cley next the Sea, Blakeney, Morston, Stiffkey, Wells next the Sea, Warham, Westgate, Binham, Langham, Field Dalling, Bale, Hindringham, Barney, Fulmodestone, Stibbard, Guist, Twyford, Bintree, Foxley, Bawdeswell, Lenwade, Morton, Taverham, Drayton, Norwich

Tour 13 - Norwich to Cockley Cley & King's Lynn
Easton, Barford, Kimberley, Hackford, Hingham, Scoulton, Watton, Little Cressingham, Bodney, Hillborough, Cockley Cley, Gooderstone, Oxborough, Oxborough Wood, Boughton, Wereham Stradsett, Setchey, King's Lynn

Tour 14 - King's Lynn

Tour 15 - King's Lynn to Heacham & Sandringham
North Wootton, Castle Rising, Wolferton, Shepherd's Port, Snettisham Reserve, Heacham, Snettisham, Ingoldisthorpe, Dersingham, Sandringham, West Newton, King's Lynn

Tour 16 - King's Lynn to Hunstanton & Brancaster
Hunstanton, Old Hunstanton, Holme next the Sea, Thornham,

Titchwell, Brancaster, Brancaster Staithe, Docking, Bircham Newton,
Great Bircham, Flitcham, Hillington, King's Lynn

Tour 17 - King's Lynn to Grimes Graves
Setchey, South Runcton, Southery, Feltwell, Hockwold cum Wilton,
Weeting, Brandon, Grimes Graves, Mundford, Cranwich, Whitington,
Wereham, Stradsett, Setchey, King's Lynn

Tour 18 - King's Lynn to Wisbech & Swaffham
Tilney High End, Terrington St John, Walpole Highway, Wisbech,
Elm, Outwell, Nordelph, Downham Market, Bexwell, Stradsett,
Fincham, Swaffham, Narborough, West Bilney, East Winch,
Middleton, King's Lynn

Tour 19 - King's Lynn to Burnham
Hillington, West Rudham, East Rudham, Tattersett, Stanhoe,
Burnham Deepdale, Burnham Norton, Burnham Overy Staithe,
Burnham Overy Town, Burnham Thorpe, Burnham Market,
Holkham, North Creake, South Creake, Sculthorpe, East Rudham,
King's Lynn

Tour 20 - King's Lynn to Walsingham
Middleton, East Winch, West Bilney, West Acre, South Acre, Castle
Acre, Great Massingham, Hellhoughton, Tatterford, Dunton,
Sculthorpe, East Barsham, Houghton St Giles, Great & Little
Walsingham, Great Snoring, Thursford, Tattersett, East Rudham,
West Rudham, Hillington, King's Lynn

TOUR 1

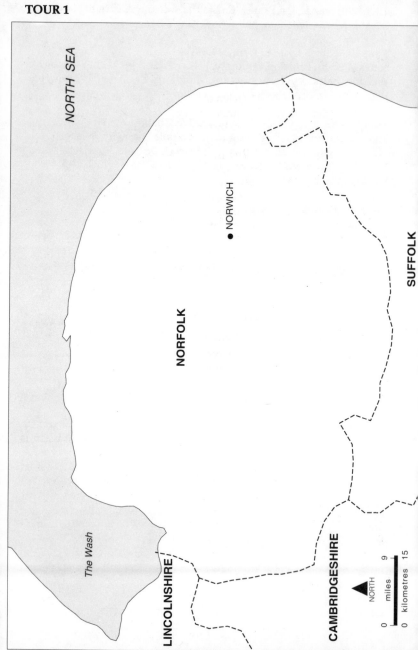

TOURS

Tour 1 - Norwich

Norwich emerged under the reign of King Athelstan in the 10th century, and during the Norman Conquest was a city with a population of about 5500. It was a major wool centre by the end of the 14th century.

Norwich is a clean and tidy city with lots of little alleys packed with shops. Market day is Tuesday in the square and the stalls are under cover and well worth a visit.

Location: On the A11, 43 miles north of Ipswich.

Information Centre: The Guildhall, Gaol Hill, ph (01603) 666 071.

Hospital: Norfolk and Norwich Hospital.

Police: Bethel Street.

Market Days: Monday to Saturday.

Early Closing Day: Thursday in winter.

Annual Events: Lord Mayor's Parade - Spring Bank holiday.
Norfolk Show in June.
Music Festival in May.

Places To See

Castle and Museum, Castle Meadow, ph (01603) 223 624. Open Monday to Saturday 10am to 5pm and Sunday 2pm to 5pm.

The castle dates from the 12th century. The keep is now a museum and has fine collections of porcelain, musical instruments and works by local artists. The River Wensum formed a natural defence from invaders on three sides. There were 10 fortified gateways and the dungeons have death masks of executed prisoners.

St Peter Hungate Museum and Brass Rubbing Centre, Princes Street, ph (01603) 667 231. Open Monday to Saturday 10am to 5pm. Admission is free.

The Museum is a former 15th century church standing in the heart of old Norwich close to the Cathedral. There are some wonderful treasures on display, and visitors can try brass rubbing which is great fun. Materials and instructions are provided for a modest charge.

Strangers' Hall Museum, Charing Cross, ph (01603) 667 229. Open Monday to Saturday 10am to 5pm.

A fascinating and historic house that dates back to 1320, the museum's collection of original costumes, dolls and toys and period rooms are just part of the attractions.

Royal Norfolk Regiment Museum, Market Avenue, ph (01603) 223 649. Open Monday to Saturday 10am to 5pm and Sunday 2pm to 5pm.

The Museum's exhibits follow the lives of soldiers in a county regiment in peace and war from 1685 to the present day. Visitors are taken on a global tour from Afghanistan to South Africa, India to America and many other exotic places.

Guildhall, Market Place, was built in the 15th century and restored in the 19th century. One of the prize exhibits is the Spanish general's sword presented to the city by Horatio Nelson in 1797.

The Cathedral is open daily from 7.30am to 6pm mid-September to mid-May, until 7pm mid-May to mid-September.

The Norman cathedral was founded in 1096 by Herbert de Losinga. The interior has some very interesting features including:

The *Nave* with its 15th century carvings (bosses) up in the roof showing stories from the Bible. You may be able to see the bosses showing the Crucifixion of Our Lord and Pharoah's Army drowning in the Red Sea. The wide pillars and round arches are typical of the Norman style of architecture.

St Andrew's Church and *St Catherine's Chapel* are reserved for prayer and silence.

The *stalls* (seats in the choir) were also built in the 15th century. Some of the tip-up seats (misericords) are left up so that you can see the carvings underneath. **Please do not lift any misericords without permission.** In the roof above the choir is a boss showing Noah's Ark.

The Bishop's Ancient Throne can be seen up the steps behind the High Altar.

Behind the altar in *St Luke's Chapel* is the *Depenser Reredos*. This profound work is a fine example of the East Anglian School of Painting.

The modern glass window in the *Bauchon Lady Chapel* depicts some of the great Benedictine monks and saints, including Herbert de Losinga, the founder of the Cathedral. Julian of Norwich is also pictured.

Before the Reformation the *Cloisters* were the centre of the life of the Benedictine monks who cared for the cathedral. Here they studied, and doorways led to the places where they ate, slept, and met visitors.

To find *Edith Cavell's Grave*, turn left outside the south door of the cathedral.

Fairhaven Garden Trust, South Walsham, is 9 miles north-east of Norwich, ph (01603) 270 449. Open from Easter to October.

The Gardens offer over 174 acres of fantastic natural woodland and water gardens, and have many rare and exotic plants and a King Oak tree said to be over 900 years old. The *Lady Beatrice* a vintage style river boat runs trips every half hour on the two South Walsham Broads from within the gardens on all open days.

Church of St Peter Mancroft is Perpendicular and the bells are dated from the 1588 Spanish Armada.

The *Coach and Horses*, a short walk from the market place, is a delightful 16th century pub that offers traditional country atmosphere and great wholesome homemade meals.

Golf: *Barnham Broom Hotel, Golf and Country Club*, Honingham Road, Barnham Broom, ph (01603) 759 393. Two 18-hole golf courses. Restrictions apply, the hire of clubs is available for overseas visitors.

Eaton Golf Club, Newmarket Road. An undulating old established 18-hole course. Restrictions apply and visitors allowed only after 11.30am, own golf clubs are necessary as is a handicap certificate.

Royal Norwich Golf Club, Drayton High Road, Hellesdon, ph (01603) 429 928. 18 holes undulating parkland course. Restrictions apply, must have a handicap certificate, essential to already belong to a golf club.

Bicycle Hire: *Just Pedalling*, 9 Church Street, Coltishall, ph (01603) 737 201.

Clay Pigeon Shooting: The Friendly Hotel, 2 Barnard Road, Bouthorpe, ph (01603) 741 161.

Cruises: The *Lady Beatrice*, a vintage style river boat, runs trips every half hour on the two South Walsham Broads from within the gardens of Fairhaven Garden Trust on all open days.

Once Bittern Dining afloat, 8 Coach House, Unthank Road, ph (01603) 506 355. The meals and tours offered are excellent and reasonably priced for about £35 which includes pick up and return but not wine.

Town Trails: Riverside walk is one of the prettiest along the banks of the river from Cathedral Close, past Pull's Ferry and the 13th century Bishop Bridge.

Costessey

Church of St Edmund is partly 13th century with Victorian additions. The *Medieval Hall* in Costessey Park is now ruins.

Golf: *Costessey Park Golf Club*, ph (01603) 746 333. 18 holes where non-members are welcome, own golf clubs are necessary.

TOUR 2

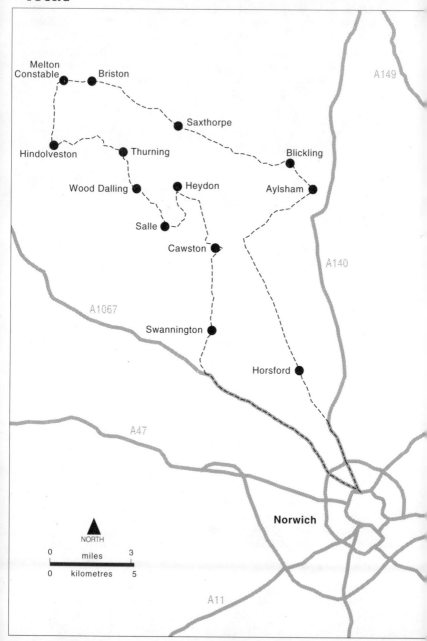

Tour 2 - Norwich Country Tour

This tour takes you along some very picturesque narrow country roads. Care should always be taken when negotiating corners, as some of the narrower roads are actually lanes and are only the same width as a car. There are always plenty of gateways and other places where cars can pull off to give way.

Leave Norwich on the A140 heading north. Near the airport, turn left onto the B1149.

Horsford

The *Church of All Saints* dates back to the 14th century and has two lovely stained glass windows.

Turn right onto the B1145.

Aylsham

A delightfully friendly and attractive small town on the River Bure. The *Market Place* in the centre is surrounded by lovely old buildings. The *Knoll* and *Bank House*, both built in 1700, are gabled. The *Manor House* is dated 1608 and *Aylsham Old Hall* 1689. The *Black Boy* is in the Queen Anne style and is a delightful pub. With wonderful little narrow winding streets, interesting shops and trading stalls on most days this is a very friendly little place where the locals will make you very welcome.

Hospital: St Michael's Hospital.

Market Days: Monday and Tuesday.

Early Closing Day: Wednesday.

Annual Events: Aylsham Show on August Bank Holiday.

The Aylsham Show is held in Blickling Park for local charities. There are trade stands, side shows and plenty of animals shown and judged.

Places To See

Blickling Hall (see Blickling for details).

Bure Valley Railway travels between Aylsham - Brampton - Buxton - Coltishall - Wroxham, ph (01263) 733 858. Open Easter to October and December, and it is best to ring for timetable.

The Railway is built on an abandoned track of the oldest East Norfolk line. The 15 inch gauge track is 9 miles long, running through some of the most beautiful and scenic countryside and the trip takes about 45 minutes. An added attraction is the *Boat Train* which combines the rail trip and a 1½ hour cruise on the Norfolk Broads. After arriving at Wroxham station a short stroll takes you to Wroxham Bridge where the boat will be waiting.

Mannington Gardens is open Sunday from Easter to October between 12 noon and 5pm; May to August on Wednesday, Thursday and Friday between 11am and 5pm.

The *moated manor house* is only open by appointment. The *Heritage Rose Gardens* have been created from an acre of walled kitchen garden and feature thousands of roses set in small gardens.

Gardens surround this lovely moated medieval manor house that is still the home of the Walpole family The ruined Saxon church is surrounded by wild flowers, and open air services are held here in the summer months. *Wolterton Park* is open daily 9am to 5pm, dusk if earlier. The *18th century mansion* is currently being restored but has some completed rooms. The gardens are also undergoing improvement and being replanted. The walks and trails in some of this beautiful countryside are magnificent.

The beautiful flint faced *Church of St Michael* dominates the market place with its 14th century tower and ten bells, which have one of the finest rings in the county. The church has a two-storeyed 1488 porch, a west gallery, stained glass windows, a 1637 pulpit and some interesting brasses.

The *Aylsham Markets* in Palmers Lane are not to be missed and are held every Monday. The sale rooms now sell everything from antiques to livestock.

Horse Riding: *Four Horseshoes Driving Centre,* Norwich/Cromer Road, ph (01263) 733 961. Open 6 days a week from Easter to October between 10am and 7pm. Be driven around 4 acres of beautiful riverside countryside, or take advantage of the driving lessons that are available.

Blickling

Blickling Hall, ph (01263) 733 084. The house is open from the end of March to the end of October on Tuesday, Wednesday, Friday, Saturday and Sunday and Bank Holiday Monday 1pm to 5pm. The Garden and Restaurant are open from 11am on the same days as the House, but open daily in July and August. The Park is open daily from dawn to dusk, and has no admission fee.

The Hall, once a dilapidated building, was bought from Sir Edward Clere in 1616 by Sir Henry Hobart. The building has been restored with the south facade looking out across the formal gardens in the Jacobean style. Domes, towers, chimneys, curved gables and a central cupola, in beautiful red brick, adorn the roof-line. The interior is mostly Georgian, but the long gallery, with its decorated ceiling dated 1620, is Jacobean. The state rooms have mullioned styled windows, fine furniture and pictures, and the tapestries are magnificent. The landscaped gardens are not as formal as they were in the 17th century, and the parkland offers fantastic walks. The Hall was left to the National Trust by the last owner, the 8th Marquis of Lothian.

The *Buckinghamshire Arms* commonly known as the 'Inn at Blickling Hall', is a beautiful 16th century pub. The meals are more than reasonably priced, and are expertly cooked and presented. Children are welcome in the restaurant and family room, and there is an outdoor play area.

Artists and photographers come from all over the world to try and do justice to the delightful mud wall and thatch cottage of *No 8* in the village. *Silvergate*. A long terrace of thatched houses makes up the hamlet near the village of Blickling.

The *Church of St Andrew* is medieval and was restored in the mid 1800s. One of the brasses belongs to that of Anne Boleyne who died in 1479.

Country Walks: There is a large area of Parkland round the lake attached to the Hall, with magnificent views of the Hall and the Mausoleum. The Orchard car park has a delightful picnic area.

Weavers Way - a 57 mile walk from Cromer to Great Yarmouth via Blickling and Stalham.

Saxthorpe

A small village where *Lound Hall* and *Mickle Hall* have been owned by the Earls of Heydon since the 17th century. The chapel of *St Dunstan* is dated prior to 1315.

Country Walks: *Mannington Hall Walks,* over 20 miles of sign-posted paths around meadows, farmland, woods and a man-made lake. The walks link up with the circular walk from Holt and the long distance Weavers Way footpath.

Craft Centre: *The Old Workshop,* The Street, Corpusty. Open Tuesday to Saturday 10am to 5pm and Sunday 12 to 5pm. A delightful complex of old buildings forming a shop, showroom and gallery around a courtyard garden selling paintings, ceramics, furniture and other fine crafts. There is a children's playground and picnic green by the river.

Briston

Delightful little village of flint and brick houses, with winding roads and lovely little cottages.

The *Green Man* is off the beaten track but is definitely worth a stop for lunch or dinner. The meals are excellent and very reasonably priced. The atmosphere is extremely friendly and hosts Doug and Pam will make you very welcome. The log fire and cosy eatery are delights for the weary traveller. Try the homemade soup and crusty rolls or the hot jacket potato with cheese, they are mouth watering to say the least.

Melton Constable

The Hall, built by Sir Jacob Astley in the 17th century, is an impressive building. The Red Drawing Room has a magnificent plastered ceiling dating from 1687. The small church of *St Peter* with its central tower is mainly Norman and stands in the grounds of the Hall.

Turn left onto country lanes then pass through Hindolveston. Turn left and pass through Thurning. Turn right for Wood Dalling.

Salle

The *Church of St Peter and St Paul* is from the 15th century. It is one of the most inspiring churches and was built by three local families, the Briggs, the Fontaynes and the Boleyns. The tower is 126ft high and the church is 171ft long with a very impressive interior that has a unique font, pulpit and wonderful woodwork. There are many brasses belonging to the families. Anne Boleyn is supposedly buried in the church but there is no documented proof.

Turn left, then left again up a 'no through' road.

Heydon

Heydon is a delightful small unspoilt village set amongst beautiful farmland and woods. One of the highlights of this village takes place at Christmas when the carollers sing on the village green. The village has a shop and post office and a blacksmith is still in attendance.

Heydon has been used for many film locations such as the cricket match in the 1970 film *The Go-Between*.

Heydon Hall, built in the 1580s, is the home of Captain William Bulwer Long who, with his family, has great success in equestrian events.

The beautiful *Church of St Peter and St Paul* stands outside the main gates to the Hall, next to the village green.

The *Earle Arms Inn*, opposite the village green, is a picturesque pub that serves great meals which are more than reasonably priced, and where the hosts, Derek and Molly, will make you most welcome.

Heading back towards Salle, turn left.

Cawston

A pretty village with one of the finest churches in the county.

The *Church of St Agnes* is Perpendicular. The west tower is very impressive and stands 120ft high. Inside is a 15th century pulpit on a stone base, a hammerbeam ceiling and some original paintings.

The *Ratcatchers* is a very popular pub and is recommended by all travellers who happen to come across it. Built in the 19th century, it offers out of this world meals (just try the grills and pies), and puddings named after characters from Dickens.

Horse Riding: *Albion Ride*, Duck Row, Cawston, ph (01603) 871 725.

Swanington

Only the chimney remains of the *Manor Farm House* built in 1650. The 1744 *Norfolk Barn*, now restored, is a restaurant and shop. The gardens are magnificent and very well laid out, with a stream, orchid houses and greenhouses. The walk through the woodland is very interesting as every season brings with it a change of flowers, shrubs and colour.

Return to Norwich.

TOUR 3

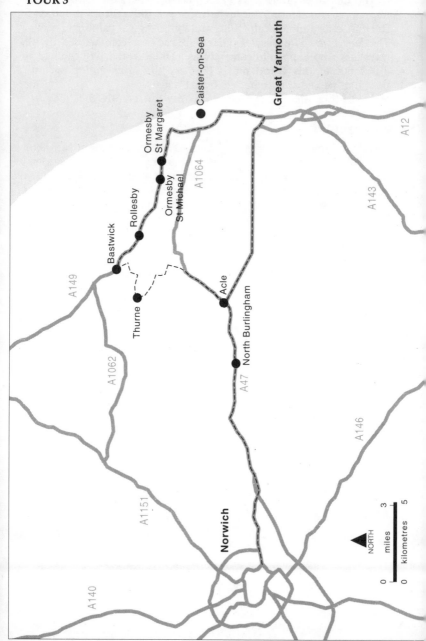

Tour 3 - Norwich to Great Yarmouth

Leave Norwich on the A47, heading east, and pass through North Burlingham and Acle.

Great Yarmouth

Tudor, Georgian and Victorian buildings makes this one of the most attractive and interesting coastal towns in England, with a golden sandy beach stretching some 5 miles. Great Yarmouth has two piers, the Wellington and the Britannia.

Location: On the A12, 20 miles east of Norwich.
Information Centre: Marine Parade, ph (01493) 842 195.
Hospital: Northgate Street, or St Nicholas' Hospital, Queens Road.
Police: Howard Street North.
Post Office: 6 North Quay and 19/20 Regent Street.
Market Days: Wednesday, Saturday and Friday in summer.
Places To See

Tolhouse Museum, Dungeons and Brass Rubbing Centre, Tolhouse Street, ph (01493) 858 900. Open June to September daily except Saturday, 10am to 1pm and 2pm to 5.30pm. October to May open Monday to Friday only 10am to 1pm and 2 to 5.30pm. Admission is free.

The Tolhouse is Yarmouth's oldest civic building, dating from the late 13th century, and it once served as courtroom and town gaol. The dungeons are a chilling experience with original cells and lifelike models. Brass rubbings of Elizabethan ladies and medieval knights are available to be tried, and the materials and instructions are included in the small charge.

Elizabethan House Museum, South Quay, ph (01493) 855 746. Open June to September daily except Saturday 10am to 1pm and 2pm to 5pm.

Built in 1596, this Tudor merchant's house is hidden behind a Georgian street front. Furnished rooms and displays illustrate home life through the ages. The panelled parlour is where the death warrant of Charles I was signed. The museum has a lovely collection of paintings, porcelain, silver, furniture and glass, and exhibitions of toys and games.

Nelson's Monument, South Beach Parade. Open July and August daily except Saturday 2pm to 6pm.

Built in 1819, this is one of Norfolk's memorials to its famous son, and at 144ft high is 41ft smaller than the one in London. Climb the 217 steps to the top where the views are magnificent.

Maritime Museum, Marine Parade, ph (01493) 842 267. Open June to September daily except Saturday 10am to 5.30pm. October to May, Monday to Friday only 10am to 1pm and 2 to 5.30pm.

The Museum is a historic Shipwrecked Sailors Home on the sea front and shows steam ships, photographs, paintings and other maritime memorabilia, including wrecks. The maritime library is available for research.

St George's Church, near the Market Square, is home to the Arts and Exhibition Centre and was built in 1713.

Greyfriars Cloisters. Open Monday to Friday daily from April to end of September from 10am to 6pm. Admission from Row 111 houses.

Remains of a 13th century friary contains some fine wall paintings which were discovered after the war.

Town Hall. Open weekdays 8.30am to 5.30pm and Friday 9am to 5pm.

Built in 1882, it contains a display of civic regalia that includes early silver maces. There is also a rare local portrait of Nelson.

Old Merchant's House, The Rows. Row 117 is a 17th century house with a fine display of 17th to 19th century wood and metalwork.

Norfolk Rare Breed Centre and Farm Museum, Decoy Farm House, Ormesby St Michael, ph (01493) 732 990. Open daily from Easter to September between 11am and 5pm.

The Rare Breed Centre has 14 rare breeds of sheep, nine rare breeds of cattle and all nine rare breeds of pigs. There are over 70 varieties of poultry, shire horses, Clydesdales, donkeys and goats. Picnic in the 17 acres of beautiful grounds, or enjoy light refreshments in the tearooms.

Butterfly Farm, on the seafront, is open from 10am March to October.

Attractions include tropical bird jungle, gardens and butterflies, fish ponds and waterfalls.

Berney Arms Windmill. Open Easter to 30 September 10am to 6pm.

The late 19th century 70 ft working marsh windmill is not accessible by road, but can be reached by boat or by rail from Great Yarmouth.

Town Wall, built between 1261 and 1400.

Craft Centres: *The Candlemaker and Model Centre,* South Market Road, Stokesby, ph (01493) 330 206. Open 7 days 9.30am till 5.30pm from early February to 24th December. Included in the price of the ticket is a free pass to the Broadland Model Railway. The Model Centre, has a large variety of handcrafted candles from all over the world. The guided tour of the workshops showing the various stages of candle-making is well worth the visit, and there are also especially imported Spanish candles. The layout for the model railways is based on the existing Norwich to Great Yarmouth line and has fantastic scenery. The *Old Stable Tea Room* offers light refreshments.

Great Yarmouth Pottery, Blackfriars Road. A large 300-year-old building built onto the 700-year-old town wall in Blackfriars Road is the family run pottery where everyone is given a warm welcome. Photographs and lovely china are on display and for sale, and take special note of the tankards which make delightful presents.

Golf: *Caldecott Hall Golf Club*, Beccles Road, ph (01493) 488 488. 9 holes, 20 bay floodlit driving range, pitching and putting greens and crazy golf. The club shop is open daily and the hire of clubs is available.

Country Walks: *Weavers Way* - 57 mile walk from Cromer to Great Yarmouth via Blickling and Stalham.

Town Trails: There are two walks around the ancient walled town, now a thriving holiday resort. Many of the old buildings were destroyed by bombing during the second world war, but many still remain.

Caister-on-Sea

Caister dates back to the 1st century AD when a small settlement was founded by the Romans. Since 1281 beacons and lighthouses have guarded the coastline.

Early Closing Day: Wednesday.

Places To See

Castle and Motor Museum. Open every day throughout the season except Saturday from 10.30am till 5pm. Children half price, under five free.

Moated castle with a 100ft tower built in 1432 on the site of a fortified manor house where Sir John Falstaff, the hero of Shakespeare's play *Henry VI*, was born. After his death in 1459 the castle became the property of the Paston family.

The car collection contains the largest private collection of motor vehicles in the country from 1893 to the present time including the first real motor car in the world, the 1893 Panhard et Levassor, with a full history. Also on display is the first Ford Fiesta and the last drophead Morris 1000.

Thrigby Hall Wildlife Gardens, Filby, ph (01493) 369 477. Open every day from 10am.

The Gardens are set in lovely landscaped surroundings and are home to many animals, birds and reptiles from Asia. There are lovely picnic areas, tree walk and swamp house.

Bygone Heritage Village, Burgh St Margaret, Fleggburgh, ph (01493) 369 770. Open Easter to October daily from 10am. November to Easter Sunday to Thursday from 10am.

The Heritage Village is set in over 40 acres of beautiful countryside with a variety of entertainment and activities that offer a great day out. Some of the attractions of this replica village include classic vehicles, village fair, pottery, saw mill, pump museum, lake, forge, vintage steam collection, fairground organs and a fire station.

The *Church of the Holy Trinity* dates from the 13th century and was once known as the parish of St Trinity.

Horse Riding: *Caister Riding School*, Beach House Farm, Yarmouth Road.

From Caister-on-the Sea take the A149 northward.

Ormesby St Margaret

A very pretty village that has two greens: one a memorial green; the other a large busy village green.

The *Church of St Margaret* is 15th century and has a Norman doorway arch and a fine west tower which houses one bell. There are some fine brasses to the Clere family dating from 1529.

Continue on through Ormesby St Michael.

Rollesby

Rollesby Broad is 1 mile south-east of the village which has a lovely Norman church.

Pass through Bastwick and Thurne. Turn onto the B1152, then turn right onto the A1064.

Acle

The village was granted permission to hold a market in the 13th century, but it is now definitely different to the cattle markets held in those days. Today's markets have a wide array of livestock and plants, and the weekly bicycle sale should not be missed.

Market Day: Thursday.

The *Church of St Edmund King and Martyr* is 900 years old and has a round tower.

The road from Acle to Coltershall was built from what was once marshlands and is a great engineering feat.

Return to Norwich on the A47.

TOUR 4

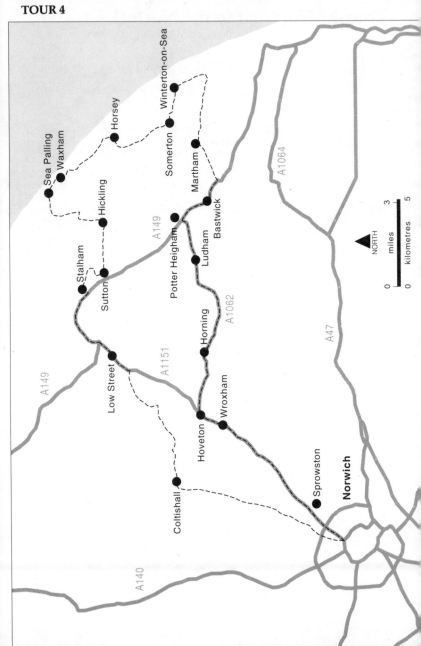

Tour 4 - Norwich to the Norfolk Broads

Travel from Norwich on the A1151 to Wroxham.

Sprowston

Country Walks: *Cottage Plantation*. Over 25 acres of woodlands, mostly larch and pine with some deciduous trees such as birch, oak, rowan, beech, sweet and horse chestnut and sycamore. The trail, marked by wooden posts with an illustration of a mouse show the directions to take. Eight trails start at the car park on Blue Boar Lane, just south of the Sprowston Garden Centre.

Golf: *Sprowston Golf Course and Driving Range*, Wroxham Road, Norwich, ph (01603) 410 657. Open 7 days a week, 364 days of the year between 8am and 9pm. 18 holes, 5982 yards, Par 70 for men and Par 71 for ladies. Pay and play, clubs available for hire, ring to book tee times for weekends. The clubhouse, restaurant and patio area are available and visitors are made very welcome.

Wroxham

Two brothers who started selling fruit to holiday makers, opened a store that is now referred to as 'The biggest Village Shop in the World'. The large Supermarket is a good place to buy groceries before taking a cruise on the Broads.

There are some beautiful old houses and a very hospitable pub right on the waterfront over the bridge in Hoveton. The bridge spanning the River Bure was built in 1614 and was widened in 1897.

Early Closing Day: Wednesday.

Places To See

Bure Valley Railway travels Aylsham - Brampton - Buxton - Coltishall - Wroxham, ph (01263) 733858. Open from Easter to October and for Santa rides in December. It is best to ring for the timetable.

The Railway is built on the abandoned track of the oldest East Norfolk line. The 15 inch gauge track is 9 miles long, runs through some of the most beautiful scenic countryside, and takes about 45 minutes. An added attraction is the *Boat Train* which combines the rail trip and a 1½ hour cruise on the Norfolk Broads. After arriving at Wroxham station take a short stroll to Wroxham Bridge where the boat will be waiting.

Barton House Railway, Hartwell Road.

The railway has a 3½ inch gauge miniature steam railway and 7¼ inch gauge riverside railway with full sized accessories. Train rides are available.

The *Church of St Mary* has many interesting features, one being the Trafford Mausoleum built in 1831.

> Turn right onto the A1062.

Hoveton

Information Centre: Station Road, ph (01603) 782 281, open summer only.
Places To See
Hoveton Hall Gardens and Grounds, ph the Head Gardener on (01603) 783016. Open Easter to mid September on Wednesday, Friday, Sunday and all Bank Holidays 2 to 5.30pm.

Very attractive grounds and gardens which provide a haven for a variety of birds and butterflies. In spring and summer the lakes and woodland are wonderful to walk around as the grounds are ablaze with colour.

The Bure Valley Miniature Railway travels between Aylsham - Brampton - Buxton - Coltishall - Wroxham.

Hoveton Broads. There are two broads, known as Great and Little.

The boundaries of both Hoveton and Wroxham meet on the lovely hump back bridge over the river Bure.

St John's 13th century church has a priest's door and a square brick tower of flint which was added later.

The *Church of St Peter* dates from 1624.

Craft Centre: *Wroxham Barns and Junior Farm*, Tunstead Road, ph (01603) 783 762. Open all year and have resident craftsmen creating unusual and stylish gifts. The Junior Farm has very friendly animals and is delightful for children of all ages. There is a small fee for entrance to the farm.

Horning

A beautiful village with interesting shops, cottages and houses. The thatched cottage right on the water offers tea in delightful gardens during the summer. Houses set in woodland have their own inlets from the river Bures.

The *Church of St Benedict* is mainly 13th and 14th century. It has some very interesting features, including the Priest's doorway which is from the 13th century, and some lovely carved pews.

Country Walks: There are broadland walks approximately 7 to 10 miles. A series of eight walks in the heart of the broadlands around Martham, Potter Heigham, Horsey, Ludham, Hickling, and Horning, How Hill, St Benet's Abbey, Tonnage Bridge and Womack Water. All walks are waymarked (signposted) and the terrain covered is varied, through villages, and along the rivers and broads.

Ludham

Very pretty and pleasant village with a nice main street, little old buildings and delightful cottages whose doorsteps open onto the road. Being surrounded by water, wherries (barges) still carry coal and other goods up the river. Boating on the river and broads is a very exhilarating experience and the sights are magnificent.

Early Closing Day: Wednesday.

Places To See

Boardman's Mill and *Clayrack Mill* at How Hill, have an open framed timber trestle windpump in working order.

St Benet's Abbey. The Abbey remains are of a monastery established by King Canute. Access is from the River Bure or the footpath.

St Catherine's Church is 15th century and is an imposing building of stone and flint. Perpendicular in style, it has a fortified clock tower. There is a 15th century crucifixion painting, an octagonal font and an ironbound poor box.

Ludham Hall is Jacobean with a Georgian facade.

Country Walks: Broadland walks approximately 7 to 10 miles. A series of eight walks in the heart of the broadlands around Martham, Potter Heigham, Horsey, Ludham, Hickling, and Horning, How Hill, St Benet's Abbey, Tonnage Bridge and Womack Water. All walks are way marked and the terrain covered is varied, through villages, and along the rivers and broads.

Potter Heigham

Delightful village with houses that open onto the road. A beautiful spot to stop and watch the boats go under the 13th century hump back bridge over the River Thurne.

The *Church of St Nicholas* has a thatched nave, chancel and a round Norman tower.

Country Walks: Broadland walks approximately 7 to 10 miles. A series of eight walks in the heart of the broadlands around Martham, Potter Heigham, Horsey, Ludham, Hickling, and Horning, How Hill, St Benet's Abbey, Tonnage Bridge and Womack Water. All walks are waymarked and the terrain covered is varied, through villages, and along the rivers and broads.

Boat Hire: *Maycraft Boat Services*, ph (01692) 670 241. Enjoy a day or an hour on the Broads with full tuition.

Turn right and pass through Bastwick, then turn left onto the B1152.

Martham

When approaching the village from any direction the 14th century *Church of St Mary* is visible standing on a small rise surrounded by ancient trees.

There are two village ponds, and a third appears after heavy rain. Ducks are well protected here because traffic signs have been erected that help the new additions to cross the roads by giving them right of way. In the summer tourists by the coach load feed the ducks and in the winter the local butcher takes over the role. Some of the locals break the ice on the ponds so that the ducks can have a swim.

Shopping in this delightful little village is a pleasure and the shopkeepers are very friendly.

There are numerous paths to walk and the River Thurne is about one mile away. Martham Broads is a very relaxing and restful place.

Country Walks: Broadland walks approximately 7 to 10 miles. A series of eight walks in the heart of the broadlands around Martham, Potter Heigham, Horsey, Ludham, Hickling, and Horning, How Hill, St Benet's Abbey, Tonnage Bridge and Womack Water. All walks are waymarked and the terrain covered is varied, through villages, and along the rivers and broads.

Bypass Newport, then turn left onto B1159.

Winterton-on-Sea

There is still a village school, post office, general store, butcher, fish and chip shop and a local fisherman who sells fresh fish from his house. A great village for getting away from it all where the coast is beautiful. There is a row of delightful thatched cottages.

The *Lighthouse*, now a private home, dominates the skyline and still reminds shipping of the treacherous North Sea.

The *12th century church*, built by the monks of St Benet's Abbey, has one of the highest towers in the county and on a clear day you can see Norwich 22 miles away.

The *Fisherman's Return*, near the village centre, is over 300 years old and was once a fisherman's cottage. It is a very popular pub with lots of atmosphere, photographs and seascapes on the walls. Meals are a treat, home cooked and very reasonably priced. Children under 14 are not permitted inside, but are welcome in the gardens in the summer.

Somerton

A small, quiet village at the eastern end of Martham Broad.

Horsey

A beautiful unspoilt little village with an inn, post box, no shops, and cottages that are delightful flint and thatch.

Horsey Windpump, open end of March to September 11am to 5pm. Closes at 6pm in July and August.

The Mill is a famous and beautiful landmark, and was built in 1912 on the site of an earlier mill.

Horsey Mere. A parcel of 120 acres of the Norfolk Broads is separated from the sea by a barrier of sand dunes, and is part of a large estate owned by the National Trust covering over 1700 acres. The Mere is a shallow broad and is ideal for fishing and sailing.

The interesting Anglo-Saxon *Church of All Saint* is thatched and has an unusual round tower.

Brograve Mill, built by Thomas Brograve, lies between Horsey and Waxham, and has a distinctive lean to it. The legend goes that this part of the country was once known as 'Devil's Country', and that after the mill was built the *devil* tried to blow it down.

Country Walks: Broadland walks approximately 7 to 10 miles. A series of eight walks in the heart of the broadlands around Martham, Potter Heigham, Horsey, Ludham, Hickling, and Horning, How Hill, St Benet's Abbey, Tonnage Bridge and Womack Water. All walks are waymarked and the terrain covered is varied, through villages, and along the rivers and broads.

Waxham

Waxham Hall is an imposing flint faced building that is believed to be the original Hall built in the 12th century. A 12ft high cobble and flint wall surrounds the property, which is not open to the public.

The *Church of St John* has been restored and has a register that dates back to 1713.

Sea Palling

This lovely little village has access to some of the most beautiful sandy beaches and outstanding natural beauty in Norfolk.

The *Church of St Margaret* is Saxon with 14th century additions. Inside the church are commemorative plaques to the lifeboats which tell of the gallant rescues by the men of Palling.

Leave on the B1159, then take the first road left.

Hickling

Pleasant village to the north of Hickling Broad where sailing, canoeing, windsurfing and other sports attract visitors. Artists love this area for both the water and the wildlife.

The *Pleasure Boat Inn* is a very popular pub.

Country Walks: Broadland walks approximately 7 to 10 miles. A series of eight walks in the heart of the broadlands around Martham, Potter Heigham, Horsey, Ludham, Hickling, and Horning, How Hill, St Benet's Abbey, Tonnage Bridge and Womack Water. All walks are waymarked and the terrain covered is varied, through villages, along the rivers and broads.

Sutton

The village is 15 miles from Great Yarmouth on the A149.

Windmill and Broads Museum, ph (01692) 581195. Open daily from 10am to 5.30pm April to September.

Built in 1789, it is the tallest windmill complete with milling machinery in the country. There is a wonderful collection of memorabilia including banknotes, wartime, medical, boots and shoes and lots of other interesting items from the past.

Craft Centre: *The Sutton Windmill Pottery*, Church Road, ph (01692) 580 595. Large range of hand-thrown Stoneware pottery.

Stalham

Very peaceful little town on the edge of the Norfolk Broads and is a centre for boat building.

Market Day: Tuesday.

Early Closing Day: Wednesday.

The thatch-roofed *The Swan Inn* in Ingham is well worth the detour. Built in the 14th century it was originally part of Ingham Priory until its destruction by Henry VIII. The accommodation is delightful with four posters, and all rooms have ensuites. Meals are excellent with either a la carte or at the bar. Outdoor patio area is ideal for warm days and there is a delightful log fire in the winter.

Country Walks: *Weavers Way* - a 57 mile walk from Cromer to Great Yarmouth via Blickling and Stalham.

Drive back to the A149 and pass through Low Street, which becomes the A1151. Take the third road on the right, passing through beautiful countryside on country roads, which are well signposted, to Coltishall.

Coltishall

Delightful picturesque village on the river Bure where nearly all the residents are direct descendants of those who lived here in the 17th century when the village prospered from brewing and boat building. There is evidence that both the Romans and Saxons had settlements here. Curved gable ends on some of the houses come from the Flemish influence which is evident all around the area. The shops are very interesting and there is a very good bric-a-brac shop in what was once an old barn.

The *Old School House* on the corner of Church Street and Rectory Road, is a wonderful red brick building with a row of dormer windows in the attic.

The *Church of St John the Baptist*, built in the 13th century, has a thatched roof, two small Anglo-Saxon windows and a 15th century tower. Beyond the ancient graveyard are water meadows and the river, and beside the church is a lovely little wood.

The *Manor House* is from the 18th century and lies behind the tall trees past the churchyard.

The *Common* is a very interesting place with seats and shady trees. Boats and yachts moor along the river banks where the ducks and other water birds wait to be fed.

The *Three Horseshoes* is a delightful 17th century thatched pub on the edge of the village. The exposed beams, collection of bottles and pictures add character to the very cosy bar. Leave space after your meal to try *death by chocolate*. It is quite superb.

Bicycle Hire: *Just Pedalling*, 9 Church Street, Coltishall, ph (01603) 737 201. Enjoy a day out in the peace and tranquillity of Norfolk's country lanes and pretty villages.

Country Walks: Take a leisurely stroll from the end of Anchor Street over the fields and water meadows to Belaugh.

Return to Norwich on the B1150.

TOUR 5

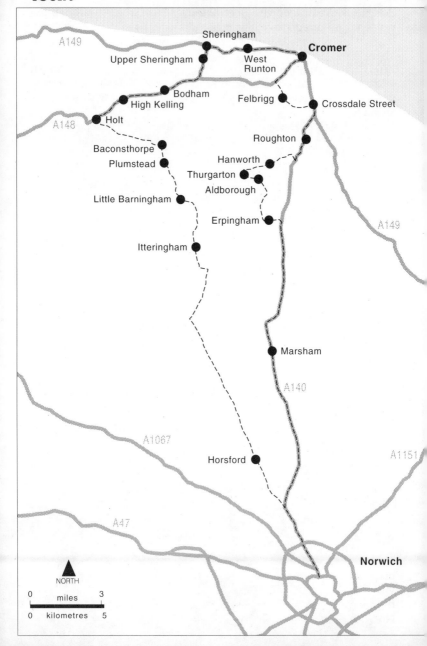

Tour 5 - Norwich to Cromer

Driving on the A140 northward, pass through Marsham, pass the Aylsham turn-off, then turn left.

Erpingham with Calthorpe

The *Church of St Mary the Virgin* was built in the mid 1300s for Sir Thomas Erpingham. The church stands on Gallows Hill surrounded by fields and is visible for miles around. There is a fine brass of Sir John Erpingham, father of Sir Thomas, who died in 1370.

Craft Centre: The craft centre is open Tuesday to Sunday (March to December) from 10am to 5pm. The Lace Museum is entirely devoted to lace and a collection of over 2000 bottles, and is closed on Saturdays. The gallery, studio workshops, tea room and gardens are all delightful.

Aldborough

The green is the main feature of this little village with 17th and 18th century shops and houses clustered around it.

St Mary's Church is dated mostly 14th and 15th century and there is evidence that a church has been here since Saxon times. There are three brasses in the church - Anne Hereward dated 1485, her husband Robert Hereward 1483, and her father Richard Randes 1493.

Thurgarton

A pretty little village of about a dozen or so small houses, with a Victorian Post Box near the crossroads. Thurgarton Old Hall dated 1733 and Thurgarton Hall are both working farms.

The *Church of All Saints* has been restored and still has a thatched roof. The interior has fine wall paintings and inscriptions.

Turn right onto country roads and pass through Hanworth, then turn left back onto the A140.

Roughton

The village boasts a supermarket, post office, service station, a fruit orchard, riding school and a bowling green. A feature of this little village is the Neolithic barrow that has been traced by crop markings from the air. A turnpike road was built in 1611, parallel to the present Norwich Road.

The *Church of St Mary* is 14th century and the round Saxon tower is notable for the inner doorway which is about 12ft from the ground.

Pass through Crossdale Street, then turn left.

Felbrigg

The town is 27 miles north of Norwich, and 2 miles south-west of Cromer, off the B1436.

Felbrigg Hall, ph (01263) 837 444. The house is open end March to end October on Monday, Wednesday, Thursday, Saturday and Sunday 1pm to 5pm, Bank Holiday Sunday and Monday 11am to 5pm. The garden is open the same days as the house but from 11am. Park Walks are available all year dawn to dusk. Park Restaurant is open end March to end October on the same days as the House 11am to 5.15pm.

The Hall, built in 1620 by William Windham, is a delightful Jacobean mansion. A new south wing was added in the late 1600s, and further additions made in 1741. The Gothic library is superb, and the Jacobean plaster ceiling in the drawing room is magnificent. There are some beautiful 18th century fine furniture, paintings and ornaments. The walled garden, the lake and the walks in the 600 acres of woodland Park renowned for beech and chestnut trees are magnificent. Photography is not allowed in the house for security reasons.

The Perpendicular *Church of St Margaret* in Felbrigg Park contains some fine 14th century brasses. One of the brasses is to Simon de Felbrigg and Roger Felbrigg and their wives. The inscription are in Norman French and are very rare, dated 1351 and 1380.

Country Walks: There are 1½ miles of lake side and 1 mile of woodland walks in the grounds of Felbrigg Hall. The circular route passes through the mature and new woodland and pasture, past the lake with wildfowl and offers a spectacular view of the Hall.

Head north onto the B1436, then turn right onto the A148.

Cromer

The prosperous town of *Shipden*, situated seaward of Cromer, slowly slipped into the sea in the late 14th century. A large rock, several hundred yards out to sea from the pier can sometimes be seen at low tides, and is known as the *Church Rock*, the remains of the church of St

Peter. Legend has it that bells from this church can be heard in stormy weather.

Location: On the A148, 25 miles north of Norwich.

Information Centre: Bus station, Prince of Wales Road, ph (01263) 512 497.

Hospital: Cromer and District, Mill Road.

Police: Holt Road.

Market Day: Friday.

Early Closing Day: Wednesday.

Places To See

The Lifeboat Museum houses models, photographs and pictures, and ship and sea memorabilia.

At *Beacon Hill*, 1 mile to the north, there are over 70 acres of iron workings from Saxon times.

The *Museum* is opposite the east end of Cromer Parish Church, ph (01263) 513 543. It is open Monday to Saturday 10am to 5pm and Sunday 2 to 4pm. Closed Monday 1 to 2pm.

The Museum is a row of old cottages with displays on the people, natural history and geology of the area.

Felbrigg Hall, 2½ miles to the south-west, is worth a visit.

The 14th century *Church of St Peter and St Paul* has a magnificent 160ft tower, the tallest in Norfolk.

A cliff path leads ½ mile east to the lighthouse, which still sends out beams to shipping.

Golf: *Royal Cromer Golf Club*, 145 Overstrand Road, ph (01263) 512 884. 18 holes, undulating seaside course alongside cliff edge. Restrictions apply.

Country Walk: *Weavers Way*, 57 mile walk from Cromer to Great Yarmouth via Blickling and Stalham.

Town Trails: Tour of the centre of this attractive little resort tells of its history as a fishing port and a holiday resort and describes some of the interesting buildings.

On the A149 coast road.

West Runton

The village is divided into two halves East and West. The flint and brick *Church of the Holy Trinity* in West Runton dates from pre-Norman times.

Norfolk Shire Horse Centre is open Easter to end of October from 10am to 5pm. Closed on Saturday except Bank Holidays. Working demonstrations are held twice a day, indoors if wet, and run for about 1½ hours. There are also wagon rides, a museum of farming equipment, picnic area and gift shop, film show of heavy horses at work. The great collection of Shires, Suffolk Punches, Clydesdales, breeds of native ponies, foals and other farm animals is wonderful.

Golf: *Links Country Park Golf Club*, ph (01263) 838 383. 9 holes, a testing downland gorse clad seaside club.

Horse Riding: *West Runton Riding Stables* are alongside the Shire Horse Centre. The Stables offer the novice or experienced rider a covered all weather riding school or accompanied rides in the beautiful surrounding countryside.

Sheringham

Upper Sheringham is on the hill, Lower Sheringham is the old fishing village. One of the most attractive small towns with a main street lined by Georgian buildings mostly built after the fire of 1708.

Location: on the A149, 27 miles north of Norwich.
Information Centre: Station Approach, ph (01263) 824 329.
Hospital: Cromer Hospital, Mill Road, Cromer.
Police: Weybourne Road.
Market Day: Saturday.
Early Closing Day: Thursday.
Places To See

Sheringham Park, off the A148 Cromer/Holt Road. Open all year dawn to dusk. Car park charge.

The Park was landscaped by Humphrey Repton in 1812 and has delightfully coloured rhododendrons that bloom late May to June and are well worth a visit. There are spectacular views of the coast and countryside from viewing towers.

Beeston Hall, 2¼ miles east. Open April to September, Friday and Sunday 2 to 5pm .

The Hall is the home of Sir Robert and Lady Preston and is set in a very picturesque park.

Beeston Priory ruins are 1 mile to the east.

North Norfolk Railway, The Station, ph (01263) 822 045.

The Railway runs steam hauled passenger trains from Sheringham to Holt on set days, taking in 5 miles of beautiful scenery. The museum houses steam railway relics.

Muckleburgh Collection on the A149, between Blakeney and Sheringham, is open daily March to October from 10am to 5pm. A free ticket to the Shire Horse Centre is presented for every two fully paid adults.

The Muckleburgh Collection is so named because it stands by the side of Muckleburgh Hill, at Weybourne Military Camp. It is the largest privately owned collection showing tanks and other armoured cars from World War II, some from the Falklands and Gulf campaigns, and some from other countries including USSR, Norway, Belgium,

Holland, France, Switzerland, Italy, Syria and Israel. There are over 100 vehicle exhibits and more than 2500 other items tracing British and County history.

There is another interesting museum to visit, that of the *Suffolk and Norfolk Yeomanry* which traces the history of these regiments since 1759. The collection is set in natural surroundings and there are working demonstrations daily in August, Bank Holidays and Sundays.

Peter's Bookshop in St Peter's Road is open every day 10am to 6pm April to October, Tuesday, Thursday, Friday and Saturday from November to March.

This bookshop is not to be missed if you are a bookworm. It has over 20,000 second hand books plus over 5000 paperbacks.

Felbrigg Hall, 4 miles south-east of Sheringham - refer to Felbrigg.

Golf: *Sheringham Golf Club*, ph (01263) 823 488. 18 holes, clifftop course. Visitors must have handicap certificates and restrictions apply.

Craft Centre: *Sheringham Pottery*, Church Street, ph (01263) 823 552. Open daily 10am to 5pm. A working pottery and craft centre where all the pottery is handmade. Well worth a visit and there is something for everyone from 50p.

Turn left onto the A148.

Upper Sheringham

Pretty little village sheltering under bracken and heather covered hills only a mile from Sheringham. Sheringham Park, Pretty Corner, flint cottages, the lovely Church of All Saint's, the *Red Lion Inn* and the reservoir make this a pleasant village to visit.

Bodham

The lovely flint *Church of All Saints* has a square fortified tower and dates back to the mid 1200s. The stained glass eastern window depicts the Nativity, Crucifixion and Ascension.

The *Red Hart*, just off the A148 is a beautiful flint and brick pub dating back to 1650. The interior is cosy with cottage style furnishings and has a lovely inglenook fireplace covered with antiques. The Inn offers homemade meals and a friendly welcome to all, including children, and the garden has a lovely barbecue area.

Continue on the A148, passing through High Kelling.

Holt

One of the most attractive small towns in Norfolk with a main street lined by Georgian buildings, mostly built after the fire of 1708. Holt is probably best known for *Greshams*, a public school founded in 1555 by Sir John Gresham, a former Lord Mayor of London. *St Andrew's Church* was also destroyed by the fire of 1708, but it was restored in 1864.

Hospital: Kelling Hospital.

Places To See

Letheringsett Watermill, is open Tuesday to Friday 9am to 1pm and 2pm to 5pm, Saturday 9am to 1pm, Sunday from May to September 2pm to 5pm. There are demonstrations on Tuesday, Thursday and Sunday 2pm to 4.30pm.

The *Holt Flyers* are horse drawn buses which run daily from the *Railway Tavern* in the town centre to the North Norfolk Railway at High Kelling, a 3 mile round trip. Enjoy tea and scones in the *Tack Room Tea Shop and Restaurant*, and see the display of old fashioned farm and driving harnesses at the Railway Tavern in the Market Place.

Bird Watching: *Lawns Hotel*, Station Road, ph (01263) 713 390.

Country Walks: *Holt Country Park*, an attractive area of mainly coniferous woodland bordering on heathland. Waymarked walks, nature trail, picnic area, wayfaring course, car park and toilets.

Town Trails: Walks around the small town, which is a conservation area, pass many attractive buildings, some made of flint.

Craft Centre: *The Old Workshop*, The Street, Corpusty. Open Tuesday to Saturday 10am to 5pm and Sunday 12 noon to 5pm. A delightful complex of old buildings forming a shop, showroom and gallery around a courtyard garden selling paintings, ceramics, furniture and other fine crafts. There is a children's playground and picnic green by the river.

Baconsthorpe

Baconsthorpe Castle, 4 miles to the south-east, is a 15th century moated, fortified house, that is now in ruins.

Plumstead

Lovely little village with brick and flint cottages. At the far end of the village is the *Olde Post Office* which bears an interesting wall painting of a Penny Black, the first adhesive stamp. The *Church of St Michael* has a 15th century stained glass window and the chancel dates from 1300.

Little Barningham

One of the few remaining unchanged villages, it is well worth the effort to stop and visit. A warm welcome in the *Old Post Office* is extended to all.

St Andrew's Church records show it has been in existence since 1320, and there is evidence that there was a Saxon church here before this one was built. Inscriptions in the church are most fascinating to read. The one below the pulpit states *Built at the coste and charge of Steven Crosbee, Anno Domino 1640* and another reads *For couples joyned in wedlocke.* The most interesting one reads *All you that doe this space pass by, as you are now even soe was I. Remember death, for you must dye and I am soe shall you be, prepare therefore to follow me.*

Pass through Itteringham back onto the B1354, then turn left onto B1149. Pass through Horsford and return to Norwich.

TOUR 6

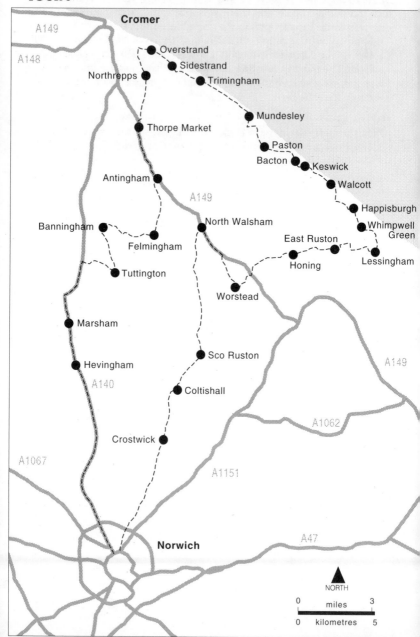

Tour 6 - Norwich to North Walsham

Drive north from Norwich on the A140. Pass through Hevingham and Marsham, then turn off to the right and pass through Tuttington.

Banningham

A lovely little farming village that has a Perpendicular flint church. The farms produce wheat, barley, sugar beet and potatoes.

Felmingham

Quaint little village set in absolutely delightful countryside. The church has a St George Cross flying and the little lane and lynch gate provide a very typical English churchyard scene. The inside of the church is well worth the stop.

Pass through Antingham and Thorpe Market.

Northrepps

Pleasant little village set in glorious countryside with a delightful Hall. There is an interesting village sign which shows a Rolls Royce Silver Ghost radiator. This sign was erected in recognition of Henry Royce of Rolls Royce fame who lived in the village whilst developing his famous car.

The *Church of St Mary the Virgin* is mainly 12th to 15th century but has parts dating back to before 1066. The weathervane is interesting as it shows a plough, an implement that played a very important part in village life.

Drive onto the coast road.

Overstrand

A pleasant seaside village that was once a fishing port. Crab fishing is still carried on and many of the locals are descendants of the original fishermen.

There are some beautiful flint cottages in the village and some of the impressive buildings were once owned by millionaires.

Overstrand Hall, next to the church, was designed by Edwin Lutyens who also designed *The Pleasaunce* a large house on the cliffs.

The 18th century *Christ Church* replaced a 14th century church that fell into the sea.

Sidestrand

The 15th century church was moved and rebuilt on its present site in 1881.

> Continuing on the coast road, pass through Trimingham.

Mundesley

Information Centre: 2a Station Road, ph (01263) 721 070, open summer only. Evidence has been found that both Romans and Saxons dwelt in this lovely fishing village that is now a holiday resort with safe swimming and lovely beaches.

Horatio Nelson was a frequent visitor to the village and stayed at the *Royal Hotel*. In the High Street is *Cowper House*, where the poet William Cowper lived in the late 1790s.

All Saint's Church, near the edge of the cliff, had been allowed to collapse into ruin by the end of the last century, but restoration work that began in 1899 has brought it back to life. Records show that there was a church here as long ago as the 11th century.

The *Royal Hotel* is elegant, tastefully furnished and has many excellent antiques. There is a restaurant and a lovely children's lounge. The menu has fresh seafood and traditional roasts.

Golf: *Mundesley Golf Club*, Links Road, ph (01263) 720 095. 9 holes, parkland course where half is reasonably flat, the other half quite hilly.

Horse Riding: *Bridge Farm Stables*, Mill Lane, Gimingham, ph (01263) 720028, is open all year. Explore beach and country lanes on hourly rides, or take holidays at their B&B accommodation with evening rides in the summer. Special ½ hour rides are available for beginners.

Paston

The village is known for its association with the Paston family who lived here in the 15th century. Letters written by John Paston and his family cover a period from 1422 to 1509, and are famous for the description of life in those days.

Paston Mill, half a mile south of Mundesley on Stow Hill, is a 19th century tower mill with working fantail and sails.

Paston Barn, near the village, is 163ft long, built of flint, and has a steeped roof. The 14th century thatched *Church of St Margaret* has some delightful wall paintings and memorials to the Paston family dated 1628 and 1632.

Bacton

The *Church of St Andrew* is about 500 years old and stands on a rise near the sea.

Bromholm Priory, or Bacton Abbey as it commonly known, was founded in 1113 as a cell to the Castle Acre Priory. Only ruins remain of the former Cluniac monastery, which supposedly was vast. Henry III visited here in 1233 and the priory was then stated to be 200ft long. The Priory is also mentioned in Chaucer's Canterbury Tales.

Bicycle Hire: *Norfolk Country Cousins*, Point House, Mill Common Road, Ridlington, ph (01692) 650 286. Explore lovely country lanes with bikes equipped with maps, panniers, locks and repair kits. Hire by the hour, day or week.

Keswick and Intwood

Keswick *All Saints' Church*, was partly dismantled for use to rebuild Intwood church. Two Halls grace the village, the Old Hall is Tudor, the new Hall was built in 1817 by Hudson Gurney.

Intwood *All Saints' Church* dates back to the 15th century. The *Hall*, originally Tudor, was rebuilt in Georgian times and now has Victorian brickwork, but the walled gardens are original. The houses near the church and the Hall vary from thatch through to Victorian. The Saxon cottage nearest to the church is the second oldest in the county.

> Continuing on the coast road, pass through Walcott.

Happisburgh

Haisbro, as it is pronounced is split into two, Upper Happisburgh where the church is, and Lower Happisburgh which runs into Eccles, another holiday village.

The famous red and white striped lighthouse built in 1791 is now privately owned and run by a trust.

St Mary's 14th century church still has shrapnel from World War II embedded in the aisle. During the same attack it lost all the windows on the south side. The tower is over 100ft high and has a fine west window. The 15th century octagonal font stands on three steps and has lovely carvings.

Hill House, a lovely Tudor house next to the church, is where Sir Arthur Conan Doyle stayed while writing *The Dancing Men*. His desk was near a window overlooking the beautiful golden sands. The self contained double room was built as a Victorian signal box, but there has never been a railway here. Now it is a very popular pub offering excellent meals and an attractive beer garden, where children are welcome.

> Pass through Whimpwell Green and Lessingham, using country lanes, and continue on to East Ruston and Honing. Then cross the A149.

Worstead

A beautiful little village set in a countryside of rich farmland, sheep and dairy herds. The famous cloth was founded here in the late 1300s when weavers used the *long staple wool* from Norfolk sheep.

The magnificent *Church of St Mary* dates from 1379, when it replaced that of St Andrew.

The *New Inn*, down a little side street, is well worth a stop and was built in 1825 in Norfolk flint.

> Turn back onto the A149, then head north.

North Walsham

Attractive village with a fountain in the centre, a few interesting shops, including a craft shop with a pink slate roof, and some charming cottages, one of which is built of stone and has a thatched roof.

Ketts is well worth a stop if you are into fish and chips, theirs are really most enjoyable.

Market Day: Thursday.

Early Closing Day: Wednesday.

Places To See

Rose Garden Centre is open all year Monday to Saturday 9am to 5pm, Sunday and Bank Holidays 10am to 5pm.

There are over 5 acres and 420 varieties of sweetly scented roses blooming in peaceful countryside, including a fascinating collection of very off beat colours such as browns, purples, greens and even grey. Attractions also include a beautiful display of shrubs, a restaurant, and a children's play area. The Gift Shop offers a wide range of pottery, pictures, books.

Kings Arms is set right on the roadside, with no pavement. It actually opens up onto the road.

Craft Centre: *Cat Pottery*, ph (01692) 402 962. Open Monday to Friday 9am to 5pm, Saturday 11am to 1pm. Fascinating and certainly a different place to visit. Walk through the buildings and see the life-like, life-sized pottery cats and dogs being made, including the glass eyes. There is also an interesting collection of railway relics and other curiosities.

Town Trails: A two hour walk around this north Norfolk market town, dating back to Saxon times. Once the centre for hand weaving in the Middle Ages, it has a variety of old and new buildings, including the school where Horatio Nelson was a pupil.

Leave on the B1150 and return to Norwich, passing through Sco Ruston, Coltishall and Crostwick.

TOUR 7

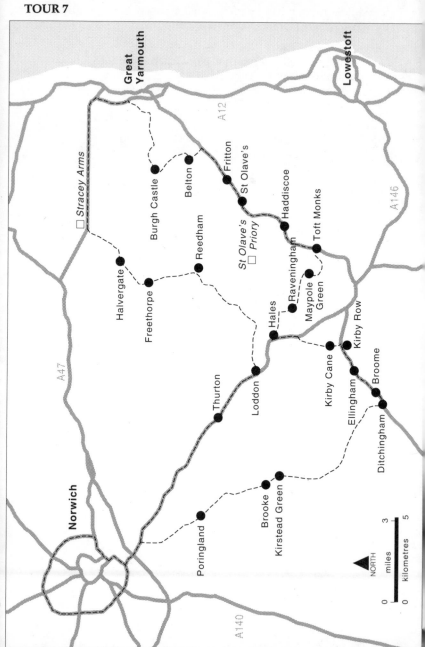

Tour 7 - Norwich to Reedham, Broads and Burgh Castle

Travel on the A146 to Lowestoft.

Thurton

St Ethelbert's, a thatched roof church that dates from 1560, has a fine Norman arched door and some interesting stained glass windows.
The *George and Dragon* is over 400 years old and still retains some beautiful old oak beams.

Take the third road on the left.

Loddon

Early Closing Day: Wednesday.
The village has many 17th and 18th century houses and one thatched cottage remains in the High Street. There are many lovely walks and picnic spots along the river's edge.
The *Church of the Holy Trinity* was built in 1492 by the Hobarts. Sir James Hobart was Attorney General to Henry VI and lived in nearby Hales Hall. The church has a beautiful stained glass window depicting crests of the wealthy families of the area.
Loddon House, an imposing building that was once a lunatic asylum, is next door to a large house built for the local doctor.
The *Angel Inn* is reputed to have been built before the church.
Craft Centre: *Loddon Water Mill Craft Centre* stands on the small bridge from Chedgrave and now houses a restaurant, coffee shop and craft centre.

Take the ferry over the River Yare.

Reedham

Location: 12 miles north-east of Norwich.
Pettitt's Animal Adventure Park, ph (01493) 700 094, is open Sunday to Friday 10am to 5.30pm, closed Saturday.
Pettitt's Feathercraft and Bird and Wildlife Park is also well worth visiting. Victor Pettitt started a small poultry business in 1921 in a disused railway carriage. In 1948 at the Norfolk show he introduced the first

frozen poultry. The picturesque park has many special attractions including wallabies, Falabella miniature horses, exotic birds, deer enclosures, vintage car rides and a half a mile of narrow gauge railway.

There is a *Taxidermist* next door to Pettitt's, where visitors can watch work in progress for museums, theatres and film companies.

The *Church of St John the Baptist* was built on the site of a Saxon church and the large Perpendicular west tower is thatched.

A chain ferry provides a vehicle link over the river Yare from Norwich to Great Yarmouth and can carry three cars at a time. The river is also crossed at Reedham by a railway swing bridge, an iron bridge built in 1846 that carries trains from Norwich to Lowestoft. This bridge is now electrically operated and swings open to let yachts pass through.

Large vessels still navigate the river and it is quite a sight to see them squeeze by the bridge as they carry fuel to the sugar beet factory at Cantley. *Briar Cottage Tea Rooms*, once the *Brickmakers Arms*, now sells delicious teas and cream scones.

The *Ship Inn* on the canal is a fabulous spot to stop or moor and enjoy a quiet pint or two. The meals are great and are reasonably priced.

The *Ferry Inn*, a 17th century pub by the river Yare, is delightful for a stopover. It has beams, a quarry tiled floor, and memorabilia adding to the charm. Meals can be taken in the restaurant, the bar or outside where you can watch the boats on the river. Children have their own sunny lounge.

Leave on the A1140, pass through Freethorpe, then take the first on the right.

Halvergate

Berney Arms Windmill is open Easter to end September 10am to 6pm, and is a late 19th century 70ft working marsh windmill. It is not accessible by road, but can be reached by boat or by rail from Great Yarmouth.

Nature Reserve: *Berney Marshes Nature Reserve* can be reached by train from Reedham or Great Yarmouth, stopping at the Berney Arms Halt. There are no public roads closer than two miles but the Weavers Way long distance footpath runs through the reserve. Seats are provided overlooking areas of grazing marsh which flood during autumn, winter and spring.

Take the country road north to join the A47.

Stracey Arms

The *Wind Pump* is a restored drainage pump. There is also an exhibition of photographs and history of windpumps.

On the A47 head for Great Yarmouth where the bypass road splits and becomes the A12 and the A143. Take the A143, then take any of the next four roads on the right. Do not go into Great Yarmouth.

Burgh Castle

The castle, built in 300AD, still has traces of Roman mortar, and the massive walls and round bastions give some idea of the strength of the original building. It was one of a chain of fortresses guarding the East Coast. Later the Normans reused it as a castle.

There is no road to the castle and the nearest a visitor can get is by foot from the church. Opposite the castle across the River Yare is the *Berney Arms* windmill, which used to grind the clinker to make cement up until the 1950s.

The *Church of St Peter and St Paul* dates from before the 11th century when the round tower was built. It still has some tiles of Roman origin. In the churchyard there is a celtic cross dated 1897 in memory of St Fursey.

The great beam in the Village Institute has an inscription carved in 1548.

Belton

The *King's Head* has seen many changes since the days of horse drawn wagons, cabs and coaches.

Turn onto A143, then turn right.

Fritton

Fritton Lake Countryworld, ph (01493) 488 208. Open every day from April to end September between 10am to 5.30pm. Free Parking.

The Park offers over 250 acres of unspoilt countryside with a large lake, gardens, 9 hole golf course, 18 hole putting lawn, adventure playground, free cart rides and coarse fishing in season. A Falconry has a flying display of Falcons, Eagles, Hawks and Owls. The Heavy Horse stables have Shire Horse and Suffolk Punches. The lakeside gardens and woodland walks are magnificent. The golf course is fringed by the woods and lake and is ideal for beginners or experienced golfers. Hire clubs or bring your own.

The Tea Room offers good teas and light meals.

St Catherine's Church dates back to the 1500s, and has two wall paintings of St Christopher and St George that were discovered in 1850.

Golf: *Fritton Lake Countryworld*, ph (01493) 488 208. 9 hole fringed woodland course suitable for beginners or experienced golfers. Hire clubs or bring your own.

Caldecott Hall Golf Club, Beccles Road, ph (01493) 488 488. 9 holes, 20 bay floodlit driving range, pitching and putting greens and crazy golf. The club shop is open daily and the hire of clubs is available.

Horse Riding: *Caldecott Hall Golf Club*, Beccles Road, ph (01493) 488 488. There are two schooling rings and over 1200 acres for hacking.

Boat Hire: *Fritton Lake Countryworld*, ph (01493) 488 208. Row boats are available for hire on the beautiful 2½ acre lake.

St Olaves

The *Windpump* is a tiny timber trestle pump that is still in working order. The *Priory*, founded in the early 14th century, has an undercroft with a brick vaulted ceiling.

Drive back to the A143 and pass through Haddiscoe.

Toft Monks

A little village, six miles south-east of Loddon, with a garage, post office, an inn, and two beautiful moated homes, one Tudor and the other timber-framed.

The *Church of St Margaret* is late 12th century and is surrounded by lovely fields. The most notable feature is the fortified Norman tower which has two windows.

Oak from the woods around the village was used to make the great doors of King's College, Cambridge.

The small village of Bulls Green, just to the north, has two timber-framed farmhouses and two Georgian houses.

Turn right for Maypole Green.

Maypole Green

This pretty little village has some farm houses and cottages of Norfolk Red brick.

Raveningham

Raveningham Gardens are extensive and surround a beautiful Georgian house.

Pass through Hales, turn onto the A146, then turn right onto the A143.

Kirby Cane and Kirby Row

The *Church of All Saints* in Kirby Cane has a round tower, a fine Stuart pulpit and a Norman doorway. Kirby Row has a row of delightful rosy red brick cottages.

Ellingham

The *Church of St Mary* in Ellingham is part 13th century with a Norman Tower. *Church Farm* was mentioned in the Domesday Book, and is still a working farm.

Turn right pass through Broome, then turn right again.

Ditchingham

Village on the banks of the River Waveney which divides Norfolk and Suffolk. The lovely 15th century *Church of St Mary* which was in the centre of the village is now stranded a fair way away surrounded by a little cluster of cottages, the *Three Bells* pub, and farmland.

Ditchingham Hall, an imposing Georgian mansion, is set in parkland designed by Capability Brown.

Ditchingham House, a quarter of a mile down the road is also Georgian but of squarer proportions. This was the home of the Victorian writer Henry Rider Haggard from his marriage in 1880 till his death in 1925. His daughter Lilias, also a writer, still lives in the house.

The Anglican *Convent of All Hallows* was founded in 1855 and the convent house opened in 1859.

Turn onto the B1332.

Kirstead Green

There are no shops in the village, which is 7 miles south of Norwich, but some wonderful houses.

Kirstead House, built in 1654, was for nearly 200 years the home of the Whall family. The tombstone of Robert who died in 1720 is the oldest in the churchyard.

The Clock House on the main road, is an interesting building with the clock on the outside wall. There are also two listed 16th century buildings, *Windetts Cottage* and *Walnut Tree Farm*.

The *Green Man House*, originally the village pub, dates back to 1700.

Langhale House is Georgian and is a reminder that there was once a hamlet of that name with its own manor and church.

Kirstead Hall, according to the Domesday Book, belonged to Bury Abbey, which Henry VIII sold to Thomas Godsalve in 1539.

The *Church of St Margaret* dates back to the 13th century, but the doorway dated 1190 is all that remains of the original building.

Brooke

The charming little Post Office has bow windows, and there is a butcher, newsagent, farm shop and two grocery shops that serve the little village lying either side of the Norwich to Bungay road. The attractive meres in the centre are home to a rare fungus. A wood in the village has the haunting name *Shrieking Woman Grove,* and the ghost of another lady is said to walk at the back of Brooke Lodge.

The Church of St Peter is about 800 years old and has a round tower topped by a lovely golden weather vane. The flint tower houses six bells which are rung regularly.

Poringland

A small, thriving village with lots of interesting little shops. In the centre lies *All Saints' Church* with its round Norman tower. Although no longer the peaceful village it once was as traffic thunders past during the day, there are still a couple of lovely quiet walks, one from the Roman Catholic church to Brooke, and the other from the Free Church takes you past the pig farm to Stoke Holy Cross.

Return to Norwich on the B1332.

TOUR 8

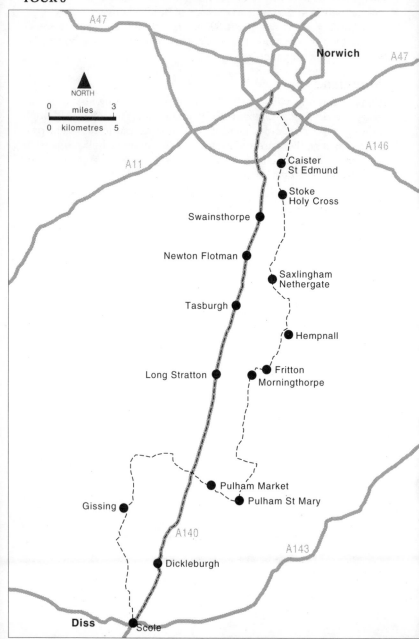

Tour 8 - Norwich to Scole

Take the ring road then take the unmarked road between the A140 and the A146. Pass through Caister St Edmund and Stoke Holy Cross.

Saxlingham Nethergate

Attractive village with thatched cottages surrounding a pretty green. The flint *Church of St Mary the Virgin* is a lovely building. The 17th century *Old Hall* and the 18th century *Rectory* make up this pleasant and friendly little village.

Pass through Hempnall and Fritton, then turn right, then left.

Morningthorpe

Pretty little village that was mentioned in the Domesday Book. The *Church of St John the Baptist* has a round Saxon tower with three bells, some stained glass and a 15th century chancel.

Pulham St Mary

The *Church of St Mary the Virgin* is a beautiful 15th century building with a west tower. Carvings on the south porch are magnificent and there are also lovely carvings on the pews and some delightful stained glass windows.
The *village school* dates back to 1670 and includes the remains of the Guild Chapel of 1401.
Horse Riding: *Waveney Valley Horse Holidays*, Airstation Farm, Pulham St Mary, ph (01379) 741 228.

Pulham Market

Attractive little village with delightful cottages around the village green. The mainly Perpendicular *Church of St Mary Magdalene*, the 16th century *Manor Farm* and the *hangar* where great airships were built make this a very diverse and interesting village to visit.
Wine: *Pulham Vineyards*, Mill Lane, ph (01379) 676 672. 12½ acres of vineyard with its own winery. Open May 1 to end of September by appointment only. Charges include guided tour of vineyard, winery and tasting. Open continuously for wine sales.

Turn left onto the A140.

Dickleburgh

Bicycle Hire: *Dickleburgh Cycle Hire*, 11 Merlewood, ph (01379) 741 510.

> Continue on the A140 then turn right onto the A143.

Scole

The *White Hart* is a lovely red brick, three storey, Dutch gabled pub built at the cross roads in 1655.
St Andrew's Church has a unique headstone commemorating the re-interment of four Christians who were originally buried in the village some 1600 years ago.

> Leave Scole on the A1066 to Diss, then take the first country road on the right, signposted Burston. Continue north and pass through Gissing, turn right onto the B1134 and rejoin the A140, then turn left.

Long Stratton

A delightful village where the new blends well with the old. The *Church of St Mary* has a Sexton's Wheel that is depicted on the village sign.

> Pass through Tasburgh.

Newton Flotman

The river Tas flows through this village and it is well worth stopping here for a browse. Stand on the bridge over the river and see *Rainthorpe Hall*, a beautiful Elizabeth mansion which is open on certain days.

Shotesham Hall stands in delightful parkland on the way back to Norwich.

Pass through Swainsthorpe, then continue on to Norwich.

TOUR 9

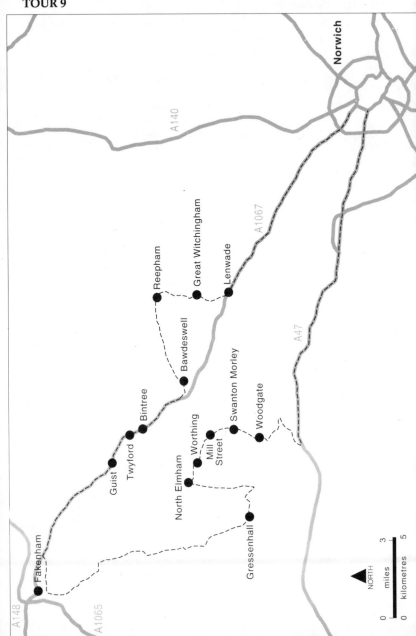

Tour 9 - Norwich to Fakenham and Gressenhall

Leave Norwich heading north-west on the A1067 and pass through Lenwade. Take the first road right signposted to Great Witchingham and Norfolk Wildlife Park.

Great Witchingham

The river Wensum flows to the south of the village, and on one side is a corn mill and on the other is the *Bridge Inn*.

Norfolk Wildlife Park is open every day of the year from 10.30am to 6pm (sunset if earlier). Saturday is children's day and up to two children per adult are admitted free.

The Park covers 50 acres and has a variety of British and European birds and animals all housed in natural surroundings. Conservation is the aim of this park and many species have been saved from extinction and returned to their native homes. Ideal day out with picnic grounds, a model farm, and a rabbit and guinea pig village, or just feed the trout in the clear water trout pool.

Great Witchingham Hall, to the south of the village, is Elizabethan, and stands in lovely parkland with the river running through the grounds. The *Church of St Mary* was built between the 13th and 15th centuries.

Head north through narrow lanes following the Reepham signposts.

Reepham

Market Day: Wednesday.

Very pretty countryside all around this attractive little market town where the two church towers welcome you.

The *Market Square* has some lovely Georgian buildings and one of them, *Dial House*, is dated 1700.

The *Church of St Mary* is unique. Not only does it serve the villages of Whitwell, Hackford and Reepham, but the chancel of the former St Michael's of Whitwell is connected by a choir vestry.

Bicycle Hire: *Windmill Ways*, 50 Bircham Road, Reepham, ph (01603) 871 111.

Leave Reepham on the B1147. Pass through Bawdeswell, then turn right onto the A1067 and pass through Bintree, Twyford and Guist.

Fakenham

Market Day: Thursday.
Early Closing Day: Wednesday.
Places To See
Pensthorpe Waterfowl Park, ph (01328) 851 465, is open all year from 11am to 5pm.

The Park is one of the largest in the world and has over 200 acres of woodland, wildflower meadows and waterside walks. There are over 100 hundred different species of waterfowl and feeding times are not to be missed.

Mill Farm Rare Breeds, Hindringham, ph (01328) 878 560, is open Tuesday to Sunday 10am to 5pm from Easter to September.

Mill Farm has over 50 breeds of rare and other farm animals set in 30 acres of beautiful countryside. There is also a Nature Trail, adventure playground and tearooms.

Raynham Hall, 3 miles to the south-west, was the home of the 18th century Viscount Townshend, known as Turnip Townshend, because of his revolutionary concept of crop rotation. The Hall still remains in the family.

East Barsham Manor, a red bricked Tudor mansion, lies 3 miles to the north.

The *Boar Inn* is a delightful country inn 4 miles to the south. It is noted for its bar food, log fires in winter and the lovely garden for hotter days.

Golf: *Fakenham Golf Club*, Hempton Road, ph (01328) 863 534. 9 holes on parkland course with water hazards. Restrictions apply.

Bicycle Hire: *Engledow's Raleigh Cycle Centre*, Creake Road, Sculthorpe, ph (01328) 864 785. Open weekdays 9am to 8pm weekends 9am to 5pm. Closed Wednesday. Over 800 cycles in stock.

Leave Fakenham and heading south on the B1146, bypass East Bilney on the left. Turn right, then first left and pass through Gressenhall Green.

Gressenhall

The village of Gressenhall is near East Dereham, 2 miles from the B1146.
Market Days: Tuesday and Friday.
Early Closing Day: Wednesday.
Places To See
Norfolk Rural Life Museum and Union Farm is open April to November, Tuesday to Saturday from 10am to 5pm and Sunday 12noon to 5.30pm. Bank Holiday Monday 10am to 5pm, ph (01362) 860 563.

One of the largest countryside collections in Britain housed in a 1777 Union Workhouse. Visit *Craftsman's Row* with its reconstructed village shop, saddler, basket maker and wheelwright workshops. *Cherry Tree Cottage* is a typical farm worker's home of the turn of the century. A Nature trail goes around the farm and along the riverside meadows.

> Leave Gressenhall on through country lanes and head for the B1110, turn left and head north crossing the B1145.

North Elmham

St Mary's Church and some lovely little cottages are set in this very friendly village, and the Cathedral grounds make an ideal spot for a picnic.

North Elmham Cathedral dates back to the 7th century and was founded by the Anglo-Saxon bishops. The Danish invasion brought about its decline. It was restored in the 10th century and left to decline again and is now in ruins.

In *Elmham Park*, across the road from the Abbey, the remains of Anglo-Saxon timber houses and burial ground have been unearthed. A footpath runs through the Park, woods and along the lakeside where the deer are delightful to watch.

Wine: *Elmham Park*, Elmham House, ph (01362) 668 571. 2½ acre vineyard with its own winery. Open all year, by appointment only. Admission charge includes tour of vineyard and slide show. Wine can be bought from the vineyard.

> North Elmham lies between the B1110 and the B1145. It is a pleasant drive to take the south-east shortcut to Worthing on the B1145. This route is well signposted. Cross the B1145, as Worthing lies on both sides of the main road. At the 'T' intersection turn left and pass through Mill Street.

Swanton Morley

The *Angel Inn* was once a cottage that belonged to an ancestor of Abraham Lincoln.

All Saints' Church was built in the late 1300s and the west tower has unique large bell openings at the top and small sound holes below.

Darby's is a very attractive red-bricked 19th century pub that was once a farmhouse. The very warm welcome received in the beamed bar with open fire and farm implements is wonderful. Meals are generous and very reasonably priced. Children are welcome anywhere on the premises, and the adventure playground, walled garden and the open fields make this pub a child's delight.

> Leave Swanton Morley on the B1147 heading south, and pass through Woodgate. Take the left country road immediately after passing through the village, which leads to the A47. Turn left onto the A47 and return to Norwich.

TOUR 10

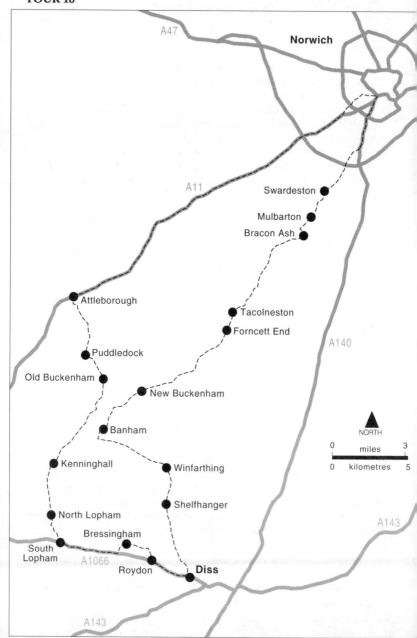

Tour 10 - Norwich to Diss

Leave Norwich on the B1113, which branches off the A140 south of Norwich.

Swardeston

The author of *Black Beauty*, Anna Sewell, was born in 1820 in the 16th century Tudor fronted cottage next to St Nicholas's Church. She died at Old Catton in 1878, six months after the publication of her book.
St Nicholas's Church was originally built in the 12th century and has a Norman tower. It was restored after World War II.

Also born in Swardeston was Edith Cavell, the nurse who was shot for assisting allied soldiers to escape from Belguim during the first world war.

Pass through Mulbarton.

Bracon Ash

The lovely flint, stone and brick *Church of St Nicholas* has a small bell tower with one bell.

Bracon Hall stands on the site of an older mansion which Elizabeth I is said to have visited.

Tacolneston

Pronounced *Takolston*, it has a delightful medieval church with pine trees, ancient gravestones and a moat on a bend in the road opposite the Old Hall. In the churchyard is a unique headstone to the memory of Mildred, wife of John Archer, departed this life aged 48 years dated 173½. Very interesting and well worth a visit.
The hill leading down to the *Manor* is surrounded by beautiful trees, and the green is surrounded by thatched cottages. The *Pelican Inn* dates back to the late 1600s.

Continue on the B1113 and pass through Forncett End.

New Buckenham

New Buckenham Castle ruins. The Castle was built 1145 and all that is left are the ruins on Castle Mound outside the village. The 17th century market house near the green is supported by wooden posts.

Banham

Banham Zoo ph (01953) 887 771, is open daily from 10am.

The Zoo has celebrated over 25 years of watching over wildlife, and being home to over 1000 animals and birds from all over the world. There are over 20 acres with special events and a very good pets corner, a must for everyone. The Woodland Walk to Monkey Island is well worth the visit especially at feeding times.

Leave Banham by either of the two scenic country roads, which are beautiful and sometimes narrow, and join the B1077. Turn right and pass through the pretty villages of Winfarthing and Shelfhanger.

Diss

Tudor, Georgian and Victorian buildings line the streets leading to the market square. Diss is set around a beautiful six acre Mere, or lake, and is a wonderful place to wander around.

Information Centre: Meres Mouth, Mere Street, ph (01379) 650 523.
Market Day: Friday.
Early Closing Day: Tuesday.
Places To See
Gissing Hall is a country mansion dating from Tudor times, and it offers B&B with luxurious rooms. It is set in five acres of magnificent surroundings, with tennis courts, croquet lawn and a large well stocked pond for fishing. The Hall is located off the B1134 near the church. The meals are delightful and include home-made produce. Children are welcome.

St Mary's Church, at the head of the triangular market place, has a tower right on the street.

Weavers Wine Bar and Eating House is a delightful historic building with a very colourful background. The exterior is as charming as the interior where the atmosphere is warm and friendly. The exposed beams have been lovingly restored, the furnishings and decor are in keeping with the character of this fantastic village. The meals are excellent and there is an extensive wine list.

Golf: *Diss Golf Club*, Stuston, ph (01379) 622 847. 18 holes and restrictions apply.

Bicycle Hire: *Dickleburgh Cycle Hire*, 11 Merlewood, Dickleburgh, ph (01379) 741 510.

Leave Diss on the A143, heading for Thetford, and pass through Roydon.

Bressingham

Bressingham Hall Gardens and Steam Museum, ph (01379) 687 386. The Steam Museum and Dell Garden are open Tuesday to Sunday early April to end of September and Sundays in October. The Hall is open on certain days.

This is a garden paradise with two main gardens that are magnificent and very colourful all year.

Dell Garden is listed as being one of the top ten gardens in England with 6 acres of 5000 different types of perennials in over 40 island beds with colour from Spring to Autumn.

Foggy Bottom Garden, so named for the mist and fog that sometimes shrouds this fantastic low lying garden, offers a back drop of Conifers to a wide variety of shrubs, perennials and grasses. Open first Sunday in the month from March to October.

The Steam Museum has historic locomotives, fire engines, steam traction engines, wagons and a Victorian steam Galloper. There are three train rides available covering a total of five miles.

The *Church of St John the Baptist* was rebuilt in 1527 and has some very interesting carved pews and a collection of shoes dated 1631.

Turn right onto the A1066.

South Lopham and North Lopham

The Lophams lay claim to three *wonders*. The first is the ford in South Lopham where the River Ouse and River Waveney begin. The second is a self grown stile, formed by a tree which has a strange shape. The third at Oxfoot Farm in South Lopham is of the Oxfoot Stone, a flattish slab of sandstone measuring 3ft x 2ft which has an impression of an ox footprint. In South Lopham *St Andrew's Church* has a most unusual tower built in the middle rather than at one end, and an Anglo-Saxon window.

Horse Riding: *Rosebrook Equestrian Centre*, South Lopham.

Continue north on the B1113 passing through Kenninghall. Take the first country road on the left and pass through some very scenic countryside, again driving along some narrow roads.

Old Buckenham

The village was mentioned in the Domesday Book and there was a castle here in 1146. A new fortress was built two miles away which is now known as New Buckenham. The earthen ramparts of both castles can still be seen.

Large groups of houses around the village green are hamlets such as *Puddledock*, *Hog's Snout* and *Loss Wroo*.

All Saints' Church is unusual as it has a thatched roof and an octagonal tower. On the north wall of the chancel is a memorial to Lionel Robinson, a wealthy businessman who lived at Old Buckenham Hall from 1906 to his death in 1922. One of his most celebrated achievements was the arranging of the 1921 Australian touring cricket team to play a representative England XI on the ground he had lovingly created from turf he had brought from Australia. Although England declared at 256 (Hobbs 85 retired hurt), rain stopped play and the match ended in a draw. The cricket ground remains today. The church also houses a bier which is thought to be one of the oldest in the country. It is oak and has collapsible handles and '1655' is carved on the side.

Leave Old Buckenham on the B1077 and pass through Puddledock on the way to Attleborough.

Attleborough

A small Saxon market town that was already established when St Edmund spent a year here preparing to become King in 856AD. The town celebrates Carnival week each June with a parade of flower floats and festivities.

Hospital: Wayland Hospital.

Market Day: Thursday.

Early Closing Day: Wednesday.

Annual Events: Carnival Week - held in June.

The *Church of St Mary* is Norman and has a 15th century rood screen and wall paintings.

Golf: *Barnham Broom Hotel*, Conference and Leisure Centre, Barnham Broom, ph (01603) 759 393. Two 18 hole golf courses. Restrictions apply.

Turn right onto the A11 to return to Norwich.

Tour 11 - Norwich to Wymondham and Thetford

> Leave Norwich on the A11 heading south.

Wymondham

Wymondham is on the A11, 9 miles south-west of Norwich. Pronounced 'Windham', the town has a very interesting past, the most famous incident being Kett's Rebellion in 1549. Two brothers, Robert and William Kett, led a revolt against the local landlords for enclosing the common pastureland. The rebellion caused such alarm that the Government in London sent two military battalions to suppress it, and the brothers were eventually executed, Robert at Norwich Castle and William in Wymondham.

Information Centre: Middleton Street.

Hospital: Norfolk and Norwich Hospital, St Stephens Road, Norwich.

Police: Avenue Road.

Market Day: Friday.

Early Closing Day: Wednesday.

Places To See

The Market Cross was built in 1617.

The *Railway Station Buffet* ph (01953) 606 433, is open for lunches and teas 10am to 5pm Monday to Saturday. Sunday teas from 2 to 5.30pm. It featured in the movie *Brief Encounter* which starred Trevor Howard and Celia Johnson. There is also a beautifully restored and converted railway carriage.

Wicklewood Mill has been restored with much of the original machinery in place.

The *Church of St Mary and St Thomas of Canterbury* was founded by the Benedictine Monks and became an Abbey in 1448.

In earlier times the twin-towered Abbey was used by both townspeople and monks, with each group allowed to use a separate half. The monks owned the nave, north-west tower and the north aisle, and the townsfolk used the remainder. This dual occupancy was caused by a feud that lasted for hundreds of years. The superb hammerbeams and Norman nave are certainly worth a visit.

The *Green Dragon* in Church Street is one of the oldest pubs in England, dating back to the 14th century. The cosy Jacobean snug still bears scorch marks from the disastrous fires of 1615.

Golf: *Barnham Broom Hotel*, Conference and Leisure Centre, Barnham

TOURS 11

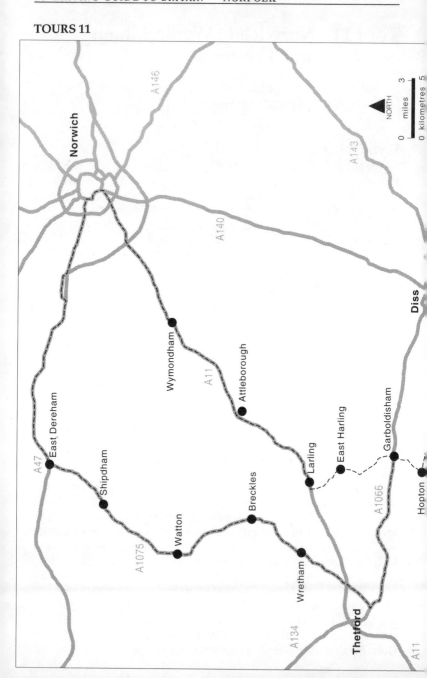

Broom, ph (01603) 759 393. Two 18 hole golf courses. Restrictions apply.
Town Trails: Walk around this old historic market town with many interesting buildings and its Abbey church dating from 1107 and an ancient timber framed Market Cross. Circular walk starts at the Market Place.

Pass through Attleborough and Larling, then turn left onto the B1111.

East Harling

The village is surrounded on three sides by farms and on the fourth side by Thetford Forest and the tiny hamlet of West Harling. It is centred around Market Street, and has some very attractive Georgian houses.

The very gracious *Church of St Peter and St Paul*, is mainly 15th century but there is evidence of an earlier church having been on the same site. The west tower has a magnificent spire, and the superb stained glass east windows have 15th century panels. There are two tombs, one dated 1435 and the other 1465.

Wine: *Harling Vineyard*, Eastfield House, ph (01953) 717 341. A 7½ acre vineyard with its own winery that is open from early May to end of October between 10.30am and 5pm. Charge includes wine tasting and refreshments. Wine can be bought in the vineyard shop. There is also a lovely picnic area.

Leave East Harling on the B1111 and pass through Garboldisham. Cross the A143 and pass through Hopton. Turn left after passing through the village.

Thelnetham

The *Windmill* in Mill Road is open July to September on Sunday 11am to 5pm. It is an early 19th century flour tower mill which works on open days, wind permitting.

Wine: *Thelnetham Vineyard*, Lodge Farm, ph (01379) 898 203. 3 acre vineyard open between 9 am and 5 pm. Admission is free and wine can be bought from the vineyard shop. The vineyard is part of a 210 acre farm with its own fishing lake.

Leave Thelnetham and return to Hopton on the B1111. Turn right and then turn left onto the A1066.

Thetford

The rivers Thet and Little Ouse meet in the centre of this charming town, once the capital for the Danes in the 9th century. In the 11th century there were 13 churches in the town and when Edward III was king there were supposedly 20.

Hospital: West Suffolk Hospital, Hardwick Lane, Bury St Edmunds.
Police: Norwich Road.

Places To See

The *Ancient House Museum* in White Hart Street is 15th century.

Castle Hill Earthworks, Castle Lane. The Castle was demolished in 1173 and the mound is all that remains.

The Priory Ruins, Water Lane, are the remains of the *Cluniac Priory of Our Lady*, founded in 1103.

Redcastle Norman earthworks in Brandon Road, the *King's House* in King Street, and the *Charles Burwell Museum* are all worth visiting.

The 16th century *Bell Hotel* is a mainly Elizabethan half-timbered building overlooking the river and a three way bridge.

Thomas Paine, the author of the *Rights of Man* and the *Age of Reason*, was born in Thetford in 1737. He migrated to America and died in New York in 1809. A statue of him stands outside the Bell Hotel.

The flint and brick *Dolphin Inn* is dated 1694.

Golf: *Thetford Golf Club*, Brandon Road, ph (01842) 752 169. 18 holes championship heathland course. Restrictions apply.

Town Trails: A two hour walk around this Breckland town that dates back to Saxon times. A variety of buildings, old and new, can be seen including the Ancient House Museum, where many of the exhibits relate to features seen on the walk.

Drive north on the A1075 and pass through Wretham and Breckles.

Watton

This lovely little village was mentioned in the Domesday Book. In the late 1100s, King John granted a market charter and one is still held here every week.

Market Day: Wednesday.
Early Closing Day: Thursday.

St Mary's Church dates back to the 12th century and has a Norman tower.

The *clock tower* in the High Street dates back to 1679. There is also a town sign in High Street taken from the legend of the Babes in the Wood.

Golf: *Watton Golf Club*, ph (01953) 881 803. 9 holes, handicap certificate required.

Country Walks: *Wayland Wood*, 34 hectares of ancient woodland, ground flora particularly good in Spring. Please keep to the tracks.

Shipdham

There were once about 20 inns along the one mile village street and as the story goes, when workers were paid on a Saturday they could be drunk before reaching home. There was once a horse-drawn fire engine and according to legend, one night a pub caught fire and one of the firemen, trying to save the beer from the burning inn, fell off his ladder and broke a leg and arm.

In *All Saints' Church* the American Stars and Stripes flag hangs alongside the British Legion flag commemorating the American Airmen from the 44th Bomber Group who were stationed at the nearby airfield.

Golf: *Swaffham Golf Club*, Cley Road, ph (01760) 721 611. 9 holes and restrictions apply.

East Dereham

A lovely little market town with a broad High Street, East Dereham is the birthplace of the poet William Cowper, in 1731. The town has some fine buildings including the *Assembly Rooms* dated 1756, *Corn Hall* dated 1857 and the *George* and the *King's Arms Hotels*. There is a lovely 13th century church overlooking the vineyard and the ruins of a Saxon cathedral in the village.

Bishop Bonner's Cottage Museum is worth a visit. Bishop Bonner was born in 1500. He was chaplain to Cardinal Wolsey and a former Bishop of London. His cottage is now home to the local museum and is notable for its pargetting, or moulded plaster decoration.

Dereham Windmill is open April to September.

There is a small picnic area in Cherry Lane which affords great views to the windmill which was built in 1836.

St Nicholas's Church is partly Norman and has two towers, one of which is a detached 16th century bell tower. The seven sacrament font is one of the loveliest in the county and it cost £12 13s 9d in 1468. The brass lectern dated 1500 and the memorial to William Cowper are all very interesting.

Golf: *Dereham Golf Club*, Quebec Road, ph (01362) 695 900. 9 holes, handicap certificate required and restrictions apply.

Reymerston Golf Club, off the B1135 between Dereham and Wymondham, ph (01362) 850 297. Superb 18 holes, 6603 yard par 72 course. Also has Pitch and Putt and a 9 hole course. Facilities are excellent.

Wine: *Elmham Park*, Elmham House, North Elmham, ph (01362) 668 571. A 2.6 acre vineyard with its own winery. Open all year, by appointment only. Admission charge includes tour of vineyard and slide show. Wine can be bought from the vineyard.

Return to Norwich on the A47.

TOUR 12

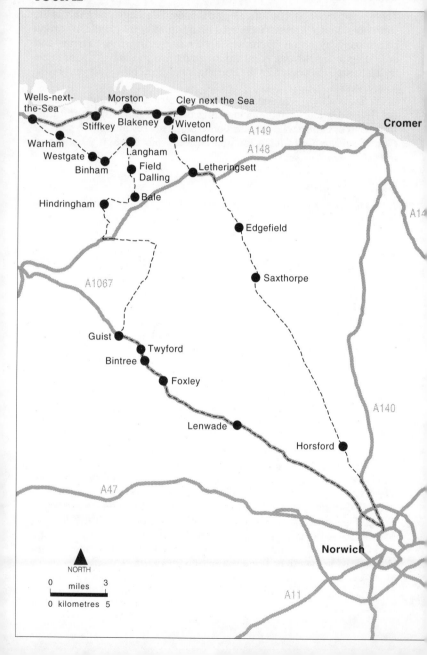

Tour 12 - Norwich to Wells-next-the-Sea

Leave Norwich on the B1149 travelling north-west, passing through Horsford, Saxthorpe, Edgefield and bypassing Holt on the A148.

Letheringsett

The bridge over the *River Glaven* was built in 1818 and is said to be the flattest in Norfolk. William Hardy did not like the road so close to his Hall, so he demolished an Inn and built tunnels under the road that are still in use today.

Letheringsett Watermill, ph (01263) 713 153, is open Tuesday to Friday 9am to 1pm and 2pm to 5pm, Saturday 9am to 1pm, Sunday from May to September 2pm to 5pm. Demonstrations are held on Tuesday, Thursday and Sunday at 2pm to 4.30pm.

The Watermill, built in 1802 of Norfolk red-brick is a fully functional water powered Flour Mill. The miller and his staff welcome visitors to demonstrations of flour making using traditional stones and water power.

Letheringsett Hall has been the home of the Hardys since the late 1700s. The *Church of St Andrew* dates back to 1300 and has lovely 16th and 17th century stained glass windows from Catton Hall in Norwich.

Continue north on the B1156.

Glandford

This is a pretty village of flint and red bricked houses that were built at the beginning of the 20th century and blend in well with the beautiful countryside.

The *Shell Museum*, ph (01263) 740 081, is open November to February, Monday to Thursday 10am to 12.30pm, March to October, Monday to Thursday 10am till 12.30pm and 2pm till 4.30pm, Friday and Saturday 2pm to 4.30pm.

The Museum was built in 1915 by Sir Alfred Jodrell and has an exotic collection of shells from all over the world. Exhibits also include jewels and pottery.

St Martin's Church was rebuilt between 1899 and 1906 in memory of Sir Alfred Jodrell's mother. There is a white marble angel and a copy of the seven sacraments font.

Bicycle Hire: *Glaven Marine*, ph (01263) 741 172. 12 speed town and trail bikes.

Wiveton

Delightful and picturesque village with cobbled flint houses.

Cley next the Sea

A small village of flint and brick houses which open up onto the street and lead to the beautiful 166-year-old windmill on the edge of the river. The river Glaven was originally tidal which brought prosperity to the village but is now just a slow moving river no more than about 20ft wide.

There is a very unusual house, *Whalebone House*, whose outside walls are decorated with sheep vertebrae.

The *Windmill* dates from 1713 and was once a corn mill. It lies between the marshes and the sea, and is open for a small fee to anyone who is game to climb to the top, where the views are magnificent. The Mill is now a Bed and Breakfast home.

St Margaret's Church is Perpendicular and overlooks the green and the valley towards Wiveton. The church dominates one end of the village and the square tower dates from the 13th century. The interior is great and the details on the woodwork and brasses are wonderful.

Craft Centre: *Made in Cley*, High Street. Open daily July, August and September. Closed Wednesday October to June. Hand-thrown domestic and sculptured pottery in stoneware and porcelain, also silver and gold jewellery all made on the premises.

Golf: *Sheringham Golf Club*, ph (01263) 823 488. 18 holes, clifftop course. Visitors must have handicaps and restrictions apply.

Royal Cromer Golf Club, 145 Overstrand Road, Cromer, ph (01263) 512 884. 18 holes, undulating seaside course alongside cliff edge. Restrictions apply.

Turn left onto the coast road, the A149.

Blakeney

This 16th century port was important for bringing salt, coal and timber to the north-east of Norfolk and for the exporting of corn. The village is one of the region's prettiest and has some fine brick and flint houses. The harbour is now a haven for sailing and pleasure boats.

The remains of the 14th century *Guildhall* are at the bottom of Mariner's Hill, and supposedly had connections with the Whitefriars. The origin of this unusual small building with its vaulted roof and tomb-like atmosphere has never been discovered.

The lovely 13th century *Church of St Nicholas* stands well away from the quay on the main coast road. The 120ft tall spire was added a century later. It also has a second tower at the eastern end which, when lit at night, would guide the ships safely into harbour. This imposing church can be seen when approaching the town from any direction.

The *King's Arms* in the village centre was a Tudor coaching inn. The restaurant is fabulous and is in a building that was once the stables. Meals are excellent and children are welcome.

The *White Horse Hotel* at the west end of the village near the quay was once three fishermen's cottages. A very popular pub serving excellent meals, and where the views over the marshes are wonderful. Children are more than welcome and there is a indoors games room for them and also swings in the garden.

Sailing: *Blakeney Point Sailing School*, ph (01263) 741 172. Beginner dinghy sailing courses in the picturesque setting of Blakeney harbour. Fully equipped shore based facilities with practical teaching on the proven Wayfarer dinghy in tidal conditions.

Tennis: *Blakeney Tennis Courts*, ph (01263) 741 106. Open 10am to 2pm Easter to end September.

Boat Hire: *Graham Bean Boats*, 69 Morston Road, ph (01263) 740 505.
   John Bean Boats, 12 The Street, Morston, ph (01263) 740 038.

Nature Reserve: Blakeney Point - open all year. Visitors please ph (01263) 740 480. April to September or (0328) 830 401 October to March to advise the Warden in advance. Access is by foot over 3½ miles or by boat from Morston or Blakeney. Car park charge at both places.

A 3½ mile sand and shingle spit is the summer home for over 11 species of seabird, including common and sandwich tern, oystercatcher and ringed plover, and about 256 other species have been spotted here. The seal colony is worth a visit and it is the first nature reserve in Norfolk to be home to both Common Seals and Grey Seals. Plant life also thrives among the sand dunes, marshlands, creeks and mudflats, with over 190 species having been recorded.

Continue on the A149 and pass through Morston.

Stiffkey

Interesting shops, including four selling antiques, add to the attractions of this little flint and brick village which should not be missed.

St John the Baptist Church is Perpendicular and the 13th century chancel was restored in 1848.

Stiffkey Hall was built by Nathaniel Bacon in the late 1500s. Only the west wing remains of the flint building that is amid the ruins of other buildings.

The *Red Lion* dates back to the 16th century and has two delightful bars with open fires. Bar meals are very good and the steak and kidney pie is wonderful and reasonably priced. The views from the patio and garden overlooking the valley are very pleasant.

Wells-next-the-Sea

The approach to the town is lined with houses that open onto the road and some lovely little shops, including an antique shop. The beach, a mile from the quay, can be reached by road, miniature railway or by walking along the embankment. Pine woods, sand dunes and a boating lake make a pleasant approach to the beach. Sailing, sailboarding and water skiing are very popular here as are bird watching and walking.

Information Centre: Staithe Street, ph (01328) 820 510, open summer only.

Market Day: Wednesday.

Early Closing Day: Thursday.

Annual Events: Regatta and Carnival at the end of August.

In the centre of the town is *The Buttlands*, a spacious rectangle village green surrounded by beautiful trees and Georgian houses. At the south-west corner a narrow passage takes you to *Ware Hall House*, a timber-framed building that was dismantled and moved from Ware in Hertfordshire.

The Victorian *Church of St Nicholas* was rebuilt in 1880.

Across the quay at the southern end of the embankment leading to the beach is the *Jubilee Cafe* which was the original lifeboat house built in 1869.

Leave Wells on the B1105, heading south, then take the first left turn.

Warham

There is a scatter of little villages known as the Warhams. On the east is Warham All Saints, and on the west is Warham St Mary. To the south is one of the best examples of Iron Age camps in England, a great earthwork in a bend of the river Stiffkey. Two high banks with a valley enclose a circle of three acres which has been preserved.

Continue on country roads and pass through Westgate.

Binham

The remains of a *Benedictine Priory*, founded in 1100, are still an impressive sight. The 13th century west front has the remains of an early tracery window, and the Norman nave now forms part of the *Church of St Mary*.

In the small village are the remains of an ancient cross.
The *Chequers Inn* is a lovely 17th century pub where the meals are very good and reasonably priced.

Leave Binham on the B1388.

Langham

Langham Fine Handmade Crystal, ph (01328) 830 511. Open daily all year except Christmas Day and Boxing Day from 10am to 5pm.

Set in a complex of 18th century red roofed barns in fantastic surroundings, a visit to this establishment is a wonderful way to spend a day. The viewing gallery, gift shop where engraving can be done while you wait, walled garden, and a large adventure playground, are just some of the attractions.
In the village is a nice little pub called the *Blue Bell*.

Leave Langham on the country road south of the village heading for and passing through Field Dalling. Still on narrow country roads, pass through Bale, then take the first or second turn right.

Hindringham

Mill Farm Rare Breeds, ph (01328) 878 560, open Tuesday to Sunday 10am to 5pm Easter to September.

The Mill Farm has over 50 breeds of rare and other farm animals set in 30 acres of beautiful countryside. There is also a Nature Trail, adventure playground and tearooms.
St Martin's Church, in the centre of the village, has records dating from 1301. The high tower and windows date from the 15th century.

Leave Hindringham heading south along country roads. Turn right onto the A148, then join the B1354 and turn right onto the B1110 to Guist. Turn left onto the A1067 and return to Norwich, passing through Bintree and Lenwade.

TOUR 13

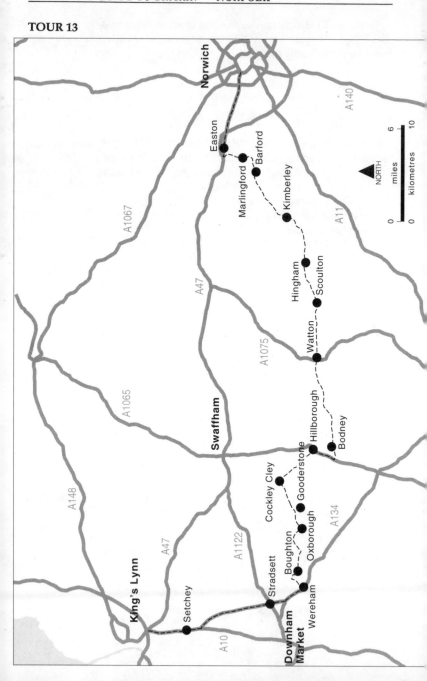

Tour 13 - Norwich to Cockley Cley and King's Lynn

Leave Norwich on the A47 heading west, turn left at Easton and pass through Marlingford and Barford. Take the first road left to join the B1108, then turn right and pass through Kimberley.

Hingham

Early Closing Day: Wednesday.

One of the most picturesque and historic little villages dating back to 925AD. The Post Office and the village green are charming and there is a *Harrods* shop. Two of the Georgian houses in this wonderful village are *Admiral's House*, and *Beaconsfield House*.

The tower of 14th century *St Andrew's Church* in the Market Square can be seen for miles around. The interior of the church has a very impressive monument dated from the 15th century to Lord Morley. The main arch of the tomb is enclosed within a magnificent framework.

Hingham was the home of Samuel Lincoln, a weaver, whose grandson was *Abraham Lincoln.* In the church is a bust of Abraham Lincoln and the village hall is also named after him.

The countryside around here is picturesque and quite unbelievable, the country lanes are narrow. Well worth the drive.

Leave Hingham on the B1108 and pass through Scoulton.

Watton

This lovely little village was mentioned in the Domesday Book. In the late 1100s, King John granted a market charter and one is still held here every week.

Market Day: Wednesday.

Earling Closing Day: Thursday.

Places to See

St Mary's Church dates back to the 12th century and has a Norman tower. The *clock tower* in the High Street dates back to 1679. There is also a town sign in High Street taken from the legend of the Babes in the Wood.

Golf: *Watton Golf Club*, ph (01953) 881 803. 9 holes, handicap certificate required.

Country Walks: *Wayland Wood*, 34 hectares of ancient woodland, ground flora particularly good in Spring. Please keep to the tracks.

> Leave Watton heading west on the B1108. At the major 'T' intersection turn right onto the A1065. Turn left for Hillborough and head in a north-west direction along a scenic country road.

Cockley Cley

The *Iceni Village Museum*, ph (01760) 721 339, is open 1st April to end of October daily 11am to 7pm.

It is a unique reproduction of a settlement of the first century AD, and is believed to be the original site of a village dating from the time of Boadicea, the Iceni queen, who led a revolt against the Romans.

There is a lovely *nature trail* along the banks of the river Gadder.

The *Museum* is set in a charming Elizabethan cottage and has a delightful collection of historical and archaeological exhibits. The half-timbered rear of the cottage makes an interesting contrast to the flint and brick frontage. The collection of carriages and farm implements is fascinating and is displayed in the old stable block.

The *Saxon church* is probably one of the oldest recorded churches, dating from about 630AD.

The *Twenty Church Wardens*, next to the church, is aptly named and delightful. The countryside around here is magnificent, peaceful and tranquil.

> Leave Iceni Village by turning left, with the church and the pub on your right. There is some fantastic scenery along these country roads. Watch out for daffodil fields in spring, and the 'Frog Crossing Warning' sign.
>
> People patrol the road between these signs and help carry the frogs from one side of the road to the other!

Gooderstone

Gooderstone Water Gardens are open daily April to October, and are delightful landscaped gardens with a lake, pools and bridges.

> Follow the well signposted country lanes.

Oxborough

Oxburgh Hall, ph (01366) 328 258, is open Easter to end October, Saturday to Wednesday 1 to 5pm, Bank Holiday Monday 11am to 5pm. The gardens are open same days as the Hall but between 12noon and 5.30pm.

The moated mansion, built in 1482 by the Bedingfield family, is a most picturesque house. The massive Tudor Gate House is very impressive and the octagonal turrets rise 80ft from the moat that surrounds the house. It did have a drawbridge but that was replaced in 1710 by a bridge. The views from the gatehouse roof across the countryside are spectacular, and the formal gardens are magnificent. The interior was remodelled to create dark richly furnished rooms. One outstanding feature is the 16th century Priest's Hole and another is the embroidery worked by Mary Queen of Scots. Photography is not allowed in the Hall.

The 19th century herbaceous borders, Victorian wilderness garden and charming woodland are all very colourful.

The *Church of St John the Evangelist* contains some fine brasses.

The old pub, the *Bedingfield Arms*, near Oxburgh Hall is lovely and worth a stop for a pint.

Turn right through Oxborough Wood.

Boughton

Very nice, quaint village with cute little workers' cottages, an old church and a lovely big pond.

Turn back onto the A134 at Wereham, then turn right and pass through Stradsett. Join the A10 and pass through Setchey to King's Lynn.

TOUR 14

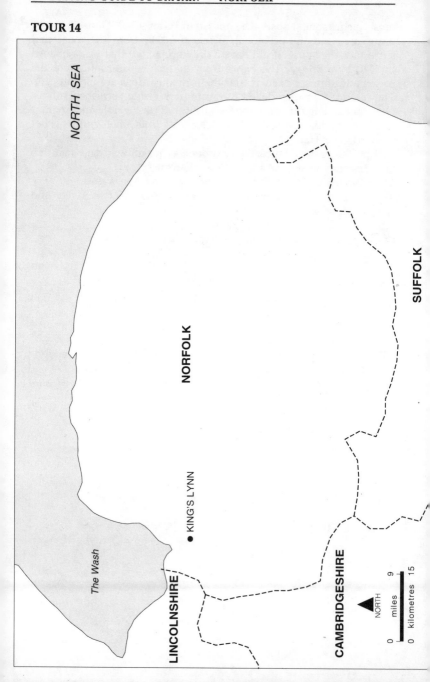

Tour 14 - King's Lynn

King's Lynn

King's Lynn is an historic town which in the past developed as a seaport. Many of the historic domestic and commercial buildings reflect its past wealth, especially during the 14th to 17th centuries.

The town has two Market Places and two medieval Guildhalls, one of which is now the Town Hall with a magnificent chequered frontage.

Information Centre: The Old Gaol House, Saturday Market Place, ph (01553) 763 044.

Hospital: Off London Road.

Police: St James Road.

Market Days: Tuesday, Friday and Saturday.

Early Closing Day: Wednesday.

Annual Events: Local fair one week mid-February.

Festival of the Arts 1st week July.

The earliest recorded performance was held in St Georges Guildhall in 1442.

Places To See

Caithness Crystal Factory, Oldmedow Road, ph (01553) 765 111. The Shop is open all year Monday to Friday from 9am to 5pm, Saturday 9am to 4pm. Glassmaking open Monday to Friday from 9.15am to 4.15pm. Easter to December on Saturday from 9.30am to 3.30pm. June to mid September Sunday 11am to 4pm. Open Bank Holidays.

The Crystal Factory is very interesting and well worth a visit to marvel at the centuries old skills of Glassmakers. There is a shop with a resident engraver and a tea room.

Clifton House is a 14th century merchant's house that has a little garden courtyard and now belongs to the council. The 16th century brick watch tower is open to the public.

St Georges Guildhall, King Street, ph (01553) 774 725, is open when not in use as a theatre, so it is advisable to phone before visiting. Monday to Friday 10am to 5pm. Saturday 10am to 12.30pm and 2 to 3.30pm.

St George's Guildhall was built about 1410 to 1420 and is the oldest surviving medieval Guildhall in England. It is a magnificent flint building. The Great Hall is 101ft long and 29ft wide on the upper floor and it still retains its original roof. Some of the rarest and finest civic treasures in Britain are housed in the undercroft, itself a prison in the 19th century. The magnificent silver and enamel King John Cup is over 650 years old; the Red Register is one of the oldest paper books in existence; and the King John Sword and four maces are among the many treasures.

The *Old Gaol House*, Saturday Market Place, ph (01553) 763 044. Open April to end October daily 10am to 5pm. November to March,

Friday to Tuesday 10am to 5pm.

The Old Gaol is certainly not for the faint hearted as you witness prison life of two centuries ago. The personal audio guide leads you to the stocks and pillory where you meet a drunken Teddy Boy locked up for the night, eavesdrop on police conversations, but most of all watch out for the rats! (not real).

Also in Saturday Market Place is the *Guildhall of the Holy Trinity*, and the *Town Hall* which was built in 1895 to match the Guildhall.

Hampton Court, in Nelson Street, was a Medieval merchant's house and warehouse.

Houghton Hall is open Thursday, Sunday and Bank Holiday afternoons from Easter until the last Sunday in September.

It is a large Palladian hall built in the 1720s for Robert Walpole, the first Prime Minister of England. There have been Walpoles in the village since the 12th century. The present owner is the sixth Marquis Hugh, Lord Great Chamberlain to the Queen. The widow of the fifth Marquis had the steps on the west front reconstructed to their original design in 1973 as a memorial to her husband. See the sixth Marquis' exceptional collection of over 20,000 model soldiers on display. The stables house Shire horses, Shetland ponies and carriages. The medieval *Church of St Martin* lies within the park.

Tuesday Market, founded in the 12th century, still holds markets in the square. *Saturday Market Place* is older than Tuesday Market and markets are held at the southern end of the High Street.

The *Church of St Margaret* is a beautiful 12th century, 235ft long, white limestone building with very impressive windows and brasses. Once part of a Benedictine priory it has an unusual tide clock.

The *Church of St Nicholas* is also very long and has a magnificent window in the west front. The font, dating from 1627, replaced an earlier one.

The *Tudor Rose* hotel near Tuesday Market Place has a 15th century house with oak beams and plenty of character. Children are welcome, and the garden is delightful.

Golf: *King's Lynn Golf Club*, ph (01553) 631 655. 18 hole woodland course. Restrictions apply.

Bicycle Hire: *Norfolk Cycling Holidays*, Sandy Way, Ingoldisthorpe, ph (01485) 540 642.

Tour 15 - King's Lynn to Heacham and Sandringham

Leave King's Lynn on the A1078 for South Wootton, the road then becomes the A148. Either take the road left in the village, or the road after the village through some of the most beautiful countryside, to see the ruins of the castle.

Castle Rising

This small village is mentioned in the Domesday Book and has a very interesting history. The 15th century Market Cross stands on the Green, west of the church.

The Norman Castle is open daily all year except Monday in winter, Christmas Day and New Years Day, ph (01553) 631 330.

Founded in 1138, it is approached through gatehouse ruins. The Keep is set within 12 acres of massive defensive earthworks once the palatial home of Queen Isabella who, after arranging for her husband Edward II to be murdered, was allowed to retire here. Climb the steep flights of stone stairs inside the Keep where the views down into the Great Hall and the surrounding countryside are magnificent.

Trinity Hospital is open Tuesday, Thursday and Saturday. On Sunday and special occasions, such as Founder's Day, the Sisters wear a long scarlet cloak with the Northampton crest and a tall black conical hat.

The Hospital, built of Norfolk red brick, was founded in the 17th century. It is arranged in a square around a grass courtyard.

The 12th century *Church of St Lawrence* has fine examples of Norman stonework on the west front and the font.

Turn left onto the A149, then turn left again on the loop road.

Wolferton

This little village is where the Royal family used to alight enroute to their country estate at Sandringham. The station was closed many years ago and is now a residence, but evidence of its historic past can still be seen.

Turn left onto the A149, then turn left for Shepherd's Port and Snettisham Reserve. Return to the A149 and turn left.

TOUR 15

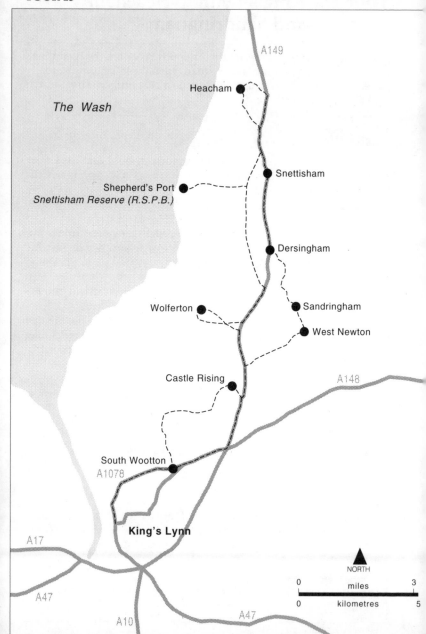

Heacham

The village sign shows a portrait of the Red Indian princess *Pocahontas* who married John Rolfe in 1614. She died at 22 and left a son who migrated to Virginia, USA. President Woodrow Wilson's wife was a descendant.

Caley Mill, Distillery, Conservatory and Herb Garden is open daily all year from 10am to 5pm. Take a trip to a lavender field during the period from mid-June to the end of the harvest in August on Monday, Wednesday and Friday.

Caley Mill is the headquarters of Norfolk Lavender and was originally a water mill. Built of local carrstone in the 19th century, it stands on a site recorded in the Domesday Book. The National Collection of Lavender has more than 50 different species. The Herb Garden has over 60 individual beds of herbs laid out like an old monastery garden, each herb having its own bed to keep it completely separate. In the centre there is a lovely locally made sun dial. The Distillery operates in July and August when the harvest is in progress. It is very interesting to watch the ancient process of extracting the tiny drops of lavender oil.

Over 100 acres of lavender fields around Heacham and at Choseley Farm, 5½ miles to the east, are best seen in July and August.

The *Church of St Mary* is 13th century with later additions. A 2ft high brass on the west wall commemorates a knight of 1485.

Return to the A149 and head south.

Snettisham

Walking around the village and along the coast is the best way to see it all.

Park Farm, ph (01485) 542 425, is open all year, daily from 10.30am to 5pm.

It is a genuine working farm with over 40 different breeds of sheep. Deer roam the park and a very pleasant way to see the park is by tractor ride. There are lovely walks and of interest is an archaeology trail. Craft workshops and a children's play area are other attractions.

The *Watermill* has restricted opening and is a charming fully restored 18th century working mill set in gardens with a waterfall.

The *market place*, in the centre of the village, has a good selection of shops, houses and a pub, all built mainly of carrstone which is still quarried. These golden brown houses are known as *Gingerbread Houses*.

The *Elizabethan Old Hall* dominates the village square and is another Sue Ryder Foundation Home. The countryside is very pretty.

Sue Ryder was the Founder and Social Worker of the Sue Ryder

Foundation for the Sick and Disabled, Co-Founder of Mission for the Relief of Suffering, and Trustee of the Cheshire Foundation. She has received the following honours: Cross of the Order of Restitution of Poland; Medal of Yugoslav Flag with Gold Wreath and Diploma; Golden Order of Merit of Poland; OBE; CMG; Baroness Ryder of Warsaw (Life Baroness); and is the author of *And The Morrow is Theirs*.

St Mary's Church is Perpendicular and the once central tower is now at the east end. The six light windows in the west end are beautiful.

Snettisham Hall, built in the 17th century of carrstone and brick, has Dutch gables over the two bays.

The *Rose and Crown* is a charming 14th century inn. The interior is delightful with open fires, barrel seats, and furnishings in keeping with the original character. Bar meals are excellent value with very generous servings.

Craft Centre: *Farmyard Craft Workshop* in the Park Farm, ph (01485) 542 425. Open daily from 10.30am.

Nature Reserve: *Snettisham Reserve and Visitors Centre* is set on the Wash with floodlit gravel pits, and is home to wintering wildfowl and summer breeding birds and migrants.

Bicycle Hire: *Norfolk Cycling Holidays*, Sandy Way, Ingoldisthorpe, ph (01485) 540 642.

Dersingham

The village is quite large and lovely and the views over the Wash and towards Sandringham woods are spectacular.

The 14th century *Church of St Nicholas* is an imposing building in a wonderful setting and is reached by an avenue of cypress trees.

Leave Dersingham on the B1440.

Sandringham

Sandringham House, Museum and Grounds, ph (01553) 772 675. The house and museum are open daily from Good Friday to the end of October from 11am to 4.30pm (Sunday from 12noon). The grounds are open 10.30am to 5pm (Sunday from 11.30am), and are closed mid-July to early August.

Sandringham Visitor Centre and Country Park is open daily from Easter to the end of October.

The country retreat of Her Majesty the Queen is at the heart of this beautiful estate that has been owned by four monarchs. It is a very imposing building where all the main rooms are used by the Royal Family when in residence. The fine collections of art and porcelain are set amongst fine furniture. The 60 acres of grounds surrounding the House have shrubs, flowers and trees and the colours are magnificent. The Museum contains displays of family photographs, vintage Daimlers and an exhibition of the Fire Brigade.

The Country Park has some beautiful nature trails, quiet picnic spots, tractor rides, orienteering and plenty of walks through woods. The *Church of St Mary Magdalene* is the Royal Parish Church and was restored in 1857. Outside the tower at the west end is a rare Greek font, over 1000 years old, that is made from one solid block of marble.

Two ancient roads cross the estate, the Icknield Way and Peddars Way.

West Newton

Behind the West Newton church is the *village hall* built in 1911 by Mrs Farr, the American wife of the Rector. During the 1930s Queen Mary had a *Little Room* added which is now used as a committee room by the Women's Institute. Both Her Majesty Queen Elizabeth and The Queen Mother attend the January meeting as members.

Country Walks: Nature Trails of 1 and 2 miles. Further information is available from the Country Park Ranger, ph (01553) 772 675.

Leave West Newton on the B1440, turn right onto the A149 and return to King's Lynn.

TOUR 16

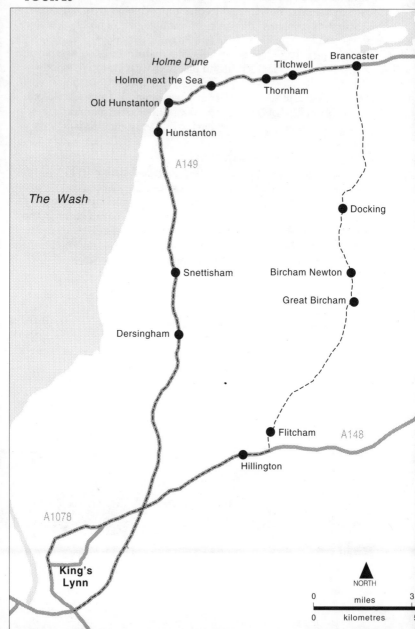

Tour 16 - King's Lynn to Hunstanton and Brancaster

Leave King's Lynn on the A149 heading north.

Dersingham

The village is quite large and lovely and the views over the Wash and towards Sandringham woods are spectacular.

The 14th century *Church of St Nicholas* is an imposing building in a wonderful setting and is reached by an avenue of cypress trees.

Snettisham

Walking around the village and along the coast is the best way to see it all. *Park Farm*, ph (01485) 542 425, is open all year, daily from 10.30am to 5pm.

It is a genuine working farm with over 40 different breeds of sheep. Deer roam the park and a very pleasant way to see it all is by a tractor ride. There are lovely walks and of interest is an archaeology trail. Craft workshops and a children's play area are other attractions.

The *Watermill* has restricted opening and is a charming fully restored 18th century working mill set in gardens with a waterfall.

The *market place*, in the centre of the village, has a good selection of shops, houses and a pub, all built mainly of carrstone which is still quarried. These golden brown houses are known as *Gingerbread Houses*.

The *Elizabethan Old Hall* dominates the village square and is another Sue Ryder Foundation Home (see p.89). The countryside is very pretty.

St Mary's Church is Perpendicular and the once central tower is now at the east end. The six light windows in the west end are beautiful.

Snettisham Hall, built in the 17th century of carrstone and brick, has Dutch gables over the two bays.

The *Rose and Crown* is a charming 14th century inn. The interior is delightful with open fires, barrel seats, and furnishings in keeping with the original character. Bar meals are excellent value with very generous servings.

Craft Centre: *Farmyard Craft Workshop* in the Park Farm, ph (01485) 542 425. Open daily from 10.30am.

Nature Reserve: *Snettisham Reserve and Visitors Centre* is set on the Wash with floodlit gravel pits, and is home to wintering wildfowl and summer breeding birds and migrants.

Bicycle Hire: *Norfolk Cycling Holidays*, Sandy Way, Ingoldisthorpe, ph (01485) 540 642.

Hunstanton

A small, well kept resort situated on the A149, 16 miles north of King's Lynn. It is the largest seaside town in North Norfolk with long stretches of sand, and is protected by cliffs of unusual stone. On the village green stands a cross which once stood in the old village.

Information Centre: The Green, ph (01485) 532 610.

Hospital: West Norfolk and King's Lynn General, London Road, King's Lynn.

Police: King's Lynn Road.

Market Days: Wednesday and Sunday.

Early Closing Day: Thursday.

Annual Event: Sailing Regatta in Summer.

Places To See

St Edmund's Church, built in 1865, has a window depicting the landing on the coast by the saint.

Lavender distillery in Heacham, 2 miles south of Hunstanton, is worth a visit.

Golf: *Hunstanton Golf Club*, Rushmere Heath, ph (01485) 532 811. 18 holes, championship links course with excellent fast greens. Restrictions apply.

Old Hunstanton

Very picturesque little village dating from 855AD when St Edmund was shipwrecked. The foundations of the coastal bridge over the river Hun are said to be Roman.

The large *Church of St Mary the Virgin* is 14th century and contains several tombs of the Le Strange family.

Grandfather's Bath in Hall Park is a spring which is the source of the river Hun.

Holme next the Sea

The *Church of St Mary* is a very impressive Perpendicular church of flint. The brick battlement was added to its tower in the late 1700s.

The town also has a *Bird Observatory and Reserve*.

Thornham

A beautiful pub called the *Kings Head* and some very old and quaint flint buildings make up this little village.

Titchwell

This is the ideal village for bird watching, golf, sailing or country walking.

The *Three Horseshoes* is a delightful country pub with a warm and cosy atmosphere and delicious homemade meals. The single large bar has lovely beams.

Nature Reserve: Bird Reserve is open daily. An attractive reserve of reed birds, salt water marshes and sandy shore. In winter there are waders and wildfowl.

Brancaster

Brancaster is a delightful little place with a lovely harbour and nature trails. *St Mary's Church* is Perpendicular and dates from the 14th century. It has a very interesting font with a cover, and three Italian lanterns.

The *Jolly Sailors* is a pleasant 200-year-old pub in the village centre. The interior is delightful with flagged floors, an open fire, and furnishings in keeping with the character of the pub adding to the cosy atmosphere. The meals are most reasonable and the homemade soups are delicious. Children are not permitted near the bar, but are welcome in the family room, outdoor play area and playhouse. Tennis courts are available.

Bicycle Hire: *Brancaster Cycle Hire*, The Dial House, The Harbour, ph (01485) 210 719. Hire a bike per hour, day or week. Tandems are available.

Nature Reserve: *Brancaster Staithe*, 1½ miles east of Brancaster, contact the Warden on (01485) 210 719 to arrange a guided tour to Scolt Head Island. The beach and tidal foreshore cover over 2100 acres and 4½ miles of sand dunes, salt marshes and a nature reserve including the site of the Roman Fort of Branodunum.

Country Walks: *Scolt Head Island Nature Trail*, nearly a mile long, is a spit of sand and shingle on the North Norfolk Coast which can only be reached by boat. It is a well known reserve for many different types of birds and plant life. Local boatmen ferry visitors to the island from Brancaster Staithe. Times vary according to the tide.

Scolt Head Island is open daily. The Reserve has extensive salt marshes and sand dunes.

Docking

There has been a village here since Roman times. There are five ponds and shops, and the lovely *Church of St Mary the Virgin,* which dates from 1588, can be seen for miles around.

Continue on the B1153 and pass through Bircham Newton.

Great Bircham

The gentle rolling countryside around this village is a haven for birdwatchers, yachtsmen and walkers.

Bircham Windmill ph (01485) 523 393, is open daily from the end of

March to the end of September, 10am to 6pm. The Tea Rooms and Bakery are closed on Saturday.

This working mill stands in the heart of fields and looks today as it must have looked over 100 years ago. The Bakery attached to the mill offers an array of fresh baked goodies. The Stables still keep ponies and sometimes there are pony rides. Sheep, hens and, of course, the miller's cat also live here.

The King's Head in the centre of this pretty village was once part of the Sandringham estates. The meals are excellent and can be served in one of three cosy little bars or in the lovely restaurant. Children are well catered for and have their own room, and there is also a large garden.

Bicycle Hire: *Bircham Windmill*, ph (01485) 523 393. All types of cycles for hire by the hour, day or week. Day routes, and green lane routes are provided.

Leave Great Bircham on the B1153 and pass through Flitcham. Turn right onto the A148, and pass through South Wootton on the return to King's Lynn.

Tour 17 - King's Lynn to Grimes Graves

Leave King's Lynn on the A10 travelling south and pass through Setchey and South Runcton. Bypass Downham Market and take the B1386 turn-off.

Southery
A village with the Great Ouse on the west and the Little Ouse to the south. The *Church of St Mary* has an impressive spire and overlooks the village. A plaque in the church contains all the names of the rectors since 1300.

Leave Southery on the B1386 and pass some of the famous fenlands, including Methwold Fens. The next road on the right (before Feltwell) will lead across and around Hockwold Fens.

Hockwold cum Wilton
The two villages seem to run into each other and are quite delightful as they nestle beside the river Little Ouse near forests and fens. There is a square stone block near the village club which is the actual dividing line.

The *Church of St James*, in Wilton, dates from the 14th and 15th centuries and has a wonderful oak roof, lovely rafters and rich carvings on the pews.

The *cross on the village green* is unusual in that it has a crown on the top.

Horse Riding: *Hockwold Lodge Riding Centre*, Cowles Drive, Hockwold, Thetford, ph (01842) 828 376.

Leave Hockwold cum Wilton on the country road travelling east towards the B1106.

Weeting
This is a Saxon village steeped in history with *Grimes Graves*, the ruins of an 11th century castle, and a 12th century boulder flint church. Surrounded by forest this area is a great base for exploring the past by foot or bicycle.

Leave Weeting on the B1106, heading south.

TOUR 17

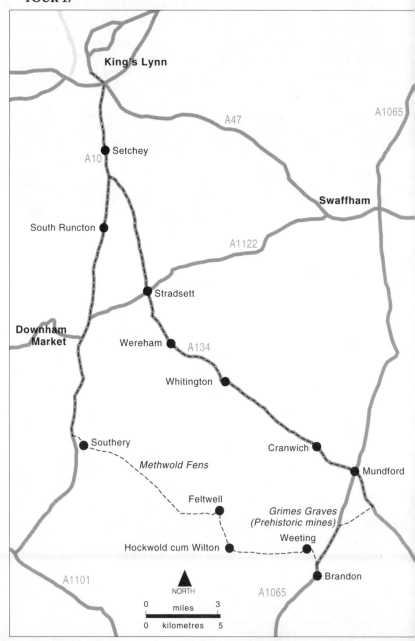

Brandon

The town, built mainly of flint, lies south-east of King's Lynn, almost on the Norfolk border, and is set on the Little Ouse river near Thetford Forest.

Market Days: Thursday and Saturday.

Places to See

Brandon Country Park was built in 1826 for Edward Bliss, and the estate then consisted of about 2500 acres. The House has been restored and is now a privately owned Hotel.

Thetford Forest Drive is open all year from 10am to 8pm or dusk if earlier.

Thetford High Lodge, located in the heart of the forest on Forest Drive, is the ideal place from which to explore Britain's largest lowland pine forest. The forest is home to four species of deer, the rare Red Squirrel and the crossbill.

Brandon Heritage Centre, George St, is open April to September on Thursday and Saturday from 10.30am to 5pm and Sunday 2pm to 5pm. October to mid December on Thursday and Saturday from 10.30am to 4pm and Sunday 2pm to 4pm.

Step back in time to the Stone Age by visiting a flintknapper's workshop and relive the town's history.

Bicycle Hire: *High Lodge Forest Centre*, Thetford Forest Park, District Office, Santon Downham, ph (01842) 815 434.

Country Walks: *Santon Downham* offers a very pleasant 2 mile walk from the Forestry Commission Headquarters through the forest of beech, pine, poplar and willow trees, to join the Thetford Road through a magnificent lime tree avenue.

Brandon Country Park, ph (01842) 810 185. 30 acres of landscaped parkland with a lake. Tree trail, forest walks and wayfaring course are open daily all year.

Boat Hire: *Bridge House Hotel*, Bridge Street, ph (01842) 813 137, for canoe/rowing boat hire on the Little Ouse River.

Leave Brandon heading north on the A11. There are plenty of signs prior to the turn-off to the right for Grimes Graves. The entrance has been preserved and is only a track leading up to the site.

Grimes Graves

Grimes Graves is not as its name suggests a burial ground, but is the site of *4000-year-old flint mines*. The approach road to the grass covered hollows is amongst pine and fir trees. One of the mine shafts is open for inspection, and is well worth the climb down the 30ft ladder to witness how miners crawled on their hands and knees with picks made from antlers to chip out the flint for tools and weapons. There are over 300 worked pits covering about 35 acres, and it is an amazing prehistoric site. The area surrounding the site is also steeped in history. The remains of *Weeting Castle* and *Weeting Heath* are not far away.

Leave the site by turning right then continuing straight ahead until the 'T' intersection. Turn left and drive along the edge of the forest, which is a military training area and is restricted. The area is well signposted back to the main road, the A11, at Mundford.

Mundford

The river Wissey meanders through the quiet beauty of the countryside. Overlooking the village green are cottages of flint with thatched roofs.

Lynford Hall has a huge estate, *West Hall* is a Tudor manor house, and with *Rosemary Cottage* are the oldest buildings in the village. *Pear Tree Inn*, now thatched cottages, is where drovers stayed and penned their stock in a small pound opposite Nelson Cottage.

The *Church of St Leonard*, built in the 13th century, has a spire that is visible from all approaches to this lovely village.

Country Walks: There are many pleasant walks, all well sign-posted, through the forest, where you will see squirrels and many beautiful birds and deer. The trees around the village are beech, and the scent and colours of these trees are wonderful.

Turn onto the A134 and pass through Cranwich, Whitington, Wereham, Stradsett and Setchey and return to King's Lynn.

Tour 18 - King's Lynn to Wisbech and Swaffham

Leave King's Lynn on the A47 heading south. Pass through the villages of Tilney High End and Terrington St John.

Walpole Highway

The village sign depicts farmland on one side and the sea wall on the other.

The *Church of St Peter* is Perpendicular, and is over 160ft long. The interior has some outstanding features, including a chandelier dated 1701, an octagonal 16th century font, a tall Jacobean font cover, and a brass eagle lectern.

Wisbech

Wisbech is on the A47, 14 miles south-west of King's Lynn. The River Nene flows through the town and its banks are lined by some fine examples of Georgian architecture. North Brink has long rows of three-storeyed red brick houses, broken by an early 18th century warehouse. The houses on South Brink are not as grand as those of North Brink.

Information Centre: District Library, Ely Place, ph (01945) 583 263.

Hospital: North Cambridgeshire Hospital, The Park.

Police: Lynn Road.

Annual Event: Blossom Tours in April and May.

Places To See

Peckover House was built in 1722 for Jonathan Peckover, a banker who founded a bank later incorporated with Barclay's Bank. The garden is magnificent and has rare trees including a very large maidenhair tree.

The *Wisbech and Fenland Museum*, beside the church, was built by George Buckler in 1846.

The *Rose and Crown Hotel* is a delightful Tudor hotel dating from the early 1600s, and has a lovely 18th century staircase.

The *Church of St Peter and St Paul* is part Norman.

In the centre of the town are beautiful Union Place, Ely Place and Crescent.

Leave Wisbech on the A1101 and head for the village of Outwell. After leaving Outwell the road becomes the A1122. Continue on this road.

TOUR 18

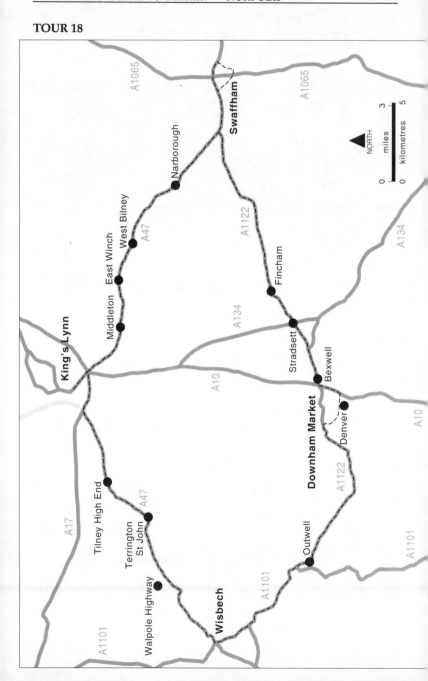

Downham Market

Market Day: Friday.
Early Closing Day: Wednesday.
A peaceful little town lying on the edge of the Fens and the River Ouse. The town has some interesting buildings and a unique *neo-Gothic clock tower* dated 1878.
The *Church of St Edmund* has a lovely spire, and the wooden 18th century west gallery has an ancient Gothic crucifix.
Golf: *Ryston Park Golf Club*, Ely Road, Denver, ph (01366) 382 133. 9 holes on flat parkland course with lake. Restrictions apply.

After visiting Downham Market, a short detour can be made to Denver, situated just off the A10, south of Downham Market.

Denver

The village has been cut in half by the A1122. The northern boundaries now belong to Downham Market. There is still a local pub, cricket club, post office/village store, a 100-year-old school and a windmill. The 13th century *Church of St Mary* stands in the centre of the village. The countryside is very pretty all around here.
Golf: *Ryston Park Golf Club*, Ely Road, ph (01366) 382 133. 9 holes on flat parkland course with lake. Restrictions apply.

Leave Denver and return to the A10. Turn left, then turn right onto the A1122 and pass through the little villages of Bexwell and Stradsett.

Fincham

An attractive little village with pretty cottages surrounded by farmland. *Playter's Hall*, *Fairswell Manor*, *Moat House*, *Talbot Manor* with its beautiful gardens, *Fincham Hall*, and a delightful green with a traditional pond make this a worthwhile stop.

The village sign outside the Old Rectory depicts Fincham Hall with the De Fincham family dressed in 16th century attire.

The *Church of St Martin* stands in the centre of the village and dates back to 1460.

Leave Fincham on the A1122.

Swaffham

Swaffham is on the A47, 15 miles south-east of King's Lynn.

The history of this charming, thriving market town lying on the northern edge of Breckland heaths and Thetford Forest is very interesting. Legend has it that the *Pedlar of Swaffham* dreamed that if he went to London he would find treasure. On his travels to London he met a man who told him that if he went to a village called Swaffham he would find treasure buried beneath a certain tree. The pedlar returned home, dug under the tree and found his fortune. The village sign is dedicated to him.

Hospital: West Norfolk and King's Lynn General Hospital, off London Road, King's Lynn.

Police: Westacre Road.

Market Day: Saturday.

Early Closing Day: Thursday.

Places To See

The triangular-shaped market place was built by the 4th Earl of Oxford in the 18th century. It has a dome-shaped roof that is topped by a statue of Ceres, the Roman goddess of harvest.

The *Museum* in the Town Hall, ph (01760) 722 922, is open Tuesday to Saturday 11am to 1pm, and 2pm to 4pm. It houses a historic display of artefacts from the stone age to modern times.

The 15th century *Church of St Peter and St Paul* is one of the finest medieval churches in East Anglia. The spire that was added in the 18th century, the double hammerbeam roof, and the carvings depicting the Pedlar of Swaffham are very interesting and well worth a visit.

Golf: *Swaffham Golf Club*, Cley Road, ph (01760) 721 611. 9 holes and restriction apply.

Leave Swaffham on the A47 heading towards King's Lynn.

Narborough

The village on the River Nar boasts traces of the Bronze Age, Iron Age and Roman occupation before being mentioned in the Domesday book. In the old part of the village, the *Ship Inn*, *All Saints' Church*, *Narborough Hall*, the *Mill*, the *Maltings* and a few other old houses are all relics of the days gone by when laden barges were the transport of the day.

Pass through West Bilney, East Winch and Middleton on the way back to King's Lynn.

---

19 - King's Lynn to the Burnhams

Leave Kings' Lynn on the A148.

West Rudham

The village, on the river Wensum, dates back to the 9th century. The barrow on the common is said to date from Neolithic times, and many finds of rough tools and worked flints have been unearthed in the local stone and gravel pits.

The *Duke's Head* is dated 1666.

The *Church of St Peter* is 13th century and has some lovely medieval stained glass windows. It merged with the *Church of St Mary* in 1720.

East Rudham

The green in the centre of this village was once owned by the Townshend family of Raynham. An Augustinian priory was founded here in the 12th century and later moved to Coxford when the Abbey was built by the De Cheney family in the 13th century. The abbey buildings were used in the late 1690s to provide material for the building of Raynham Hall. There are still some remains of the Abbey behind the farm at Tattersett.

After passing through the village of Tattersett, turn left onto the B1454. Pass through the village of Docking, then turn right onto the B1153, and head for the coast.

Brancaster

Brancaster is a delightful little place with a lovely harbour and nature trails. *St Mary's Church* is Perpendicular and dates from the 14th century. It has a very interesting font with a cover, and three Italian lanterns.

The *Jolly Sailors* is a pleasant 200-year-old pub in the village centre. The interior is delightful with flagged floors, an open fire, and furnishings in keeping with the character of the pub adding to the cosy atmosphere. The meals are most reasonable and the homemade soups are delicious. Children are not permitted near the bar, but are welcome in the family room, outdoor play area and playhouse. Tennis courts are available.

Bicycle Hire: *Brancaster Cycle Hire*, The Dial House, The Harbour, ph (01485) 210 719. Hire a bike per hour, day or week. Tandems are available.

TOUR 19

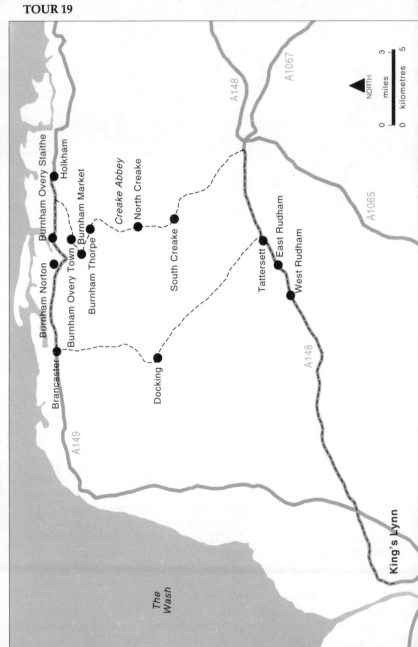

Nature Reserve: *Brancaster Staithe*, 1½ miles east of Brancaster, contact the Warden on (01485) 210 719 to arrange a guided tour to Scolt Head Island. The beach and tidal foreshore cover over 2100 acres and 4½ miles of sand dunes, salt marshes and a nature reserve including the site of the Roman Fort of Branodunum.

Country Walks: *Scolt Head Island Nature Trail*, nearly a mile long, is a spit of sand and shingle on the North Norfolk Coast which can only be reached by boat. It is a well known reserve for many different types of birds and plant life. Local boatmen ferry visitors to the island from Brancaster Staithe. Times vary according to the tide.

Scolt Head Island is open daily. The Reserve has extensive salt marshes and sand dunes.

Leave Brancaster heading east on the A149 coast road.

Burnham Norton

The town has the remains of a *Carmelite Friary* founded in 1241, and the gatehouse has some wonderful flush panelling.

The *Church of St Margaret* is unusual with a round Norman tower, a Jacobean pulpit and a square Norman font.

Burnham Overy Staithe

A small coastal village of charming cottages that is a popular sailing venue. It is situated where the River Burn runs out to the sea and where the creek winds out from the harbour between lavender covered salt marshes.

Holkham

The tiny village is part of the Holkham estate and opposite the hotel at the main entrance to the park is Lady Anne's Walk which goes along the beach to Wells.

Holkham Hall Garden and Grounds, ph (01328) 710 227. The Hall is open daily except Friday and Saturday from the beginning of June to the end of September between 1.30 and 5pm. It is also open on Bank Holidays. The Gardens are open throughout the year 10am to 5pm.

Holkham Pottery, Art Gallery and *Bygones Museum* and the *Reserve* are open daily.

Thomas William Coke built the great Palladian *Holkham Hall* in the 1730s in a park enclosed by eight miles of wall. It was inherited by his great nephew Thomas William Roberts who took the family name and became famous as the great agriculturist 'Coke of Norfolk'. In 1837 he became the Earl of Leicester. The Hall boasts some 200 years and 7 generations of living history, fine art, paintings and furniture.

The Bygones Museum has over 4000 items. The lakeside walk with acres of picnic areas and 18th century walled garden are worth visiting.

The reserve has grazing marshes, pine planted sand dunes and salt water marshes.

The *Church of St Withburga* was restored in the 1870s by Juliana, Countess of Leicester. The church had been named after one of the daughters of the family, who died in 743AD.

Country Walks: 2½ miles lake walk, 4½ miles farm walk. The two circular walks explore the surrounding park and woodland.

Leave Holkham heading south on the B1155.

Burnham Overy Town

Burnham Overy Mill is not open but is worth viewing from the outside. It is a very interesting and attractive group of red brick buildings that include a miller's house, mill workers' cottages and a barn built about 1795. The three-storeyed water mill straddles the River Burn.

Burnham Windmill is a landmark for miles.

The flint *Church of St Clement* has a square Norman central tower. The cupola was added in the 17th century. There is a small painting of St Christopher, and the Stuart table is unique and very interesting.

Burnham Market

The *Church of St Mary* in this lovely little village has a fine tower, and behind it is Westgate Hall built in 1783.

The *Hoste Arms* is a lovely large white painted pub, that has been an inn since 1650. The bars are very inviting and have lovely exposed beams and open fireplaces. Meals are of a high standard and are reasonably priced. Children are welcome in the family room and outdoor play area.

Leave Burnham Market on the country road, which is well signposted, for Burnham Thorpe and the Carmelite Friary.

Burnham Thorpe

An attractive village that was the birthplace of Horatio Nelson, son of the Reverend Edmund Nelson, rector of Burnham Thorpe Church and also Burnham Norton Church. Horatio Nelson was born on 29 September 1758, and was the fifth son of 11 children. It was after his mother died, when he was 12 years old, that he went to sea.

All Saints' Church has a marble font and many memorials to Nelson, and the lectern was made from the timbers of his ship the *Victory*.

Lord Nelson's Prayer

May the Great God, whom I worship, grant to my Country and for the benefit of Europe in general, a great and glorious victory: and may no misconduct, in any one, tarnish it: and may humanity after victory be the predominant feature in the British Fleet.

For myself individually, I commit my life to Him who made me and may his blessing light upon my endeavours for serving my Country faithfully. To Him I resign myself and the just cause which is entrusted to me to defend. Amen, Amen, Amen.

After leaving this historical village head south along the beautiful country roads for Creake Abbey, which is well signposted to the B1355.

North Creake and South Creake

The two villages are linked by the River Burn and were mentioned in the Domesday Book. The village sign on the green at South Creake has on one side St Mary's Church and a ploughman, and on the other side is a battle scene.

The Lord of the Manor is Earl Spencer of Althorpe, who lives at the family home of Althorpe in Northamptonshire. He is the brother of Diana, Princess of Wales.

Creake Abbey was home to the Augustinian canons and was a priory until 1231 when King Henry III gave it Abbey status. The remains are worth visiting.

St Mary's Church in North Creake was rebuilt in the 1450s. In West Street there is a three-storeyed tower mill that is reputedly the smallest corn mill in Norfolk. It was built in 1820.

St Mary's Church in South Creake is a mixture of Perpendicular and Decorated and has a magnificent hammer beam roof. The 15th century pulpit and brasses are very interesting.

Leave South Creake on the B1355 and at the junction with the main A148, turn right and return to Norwich.

TOUR 20

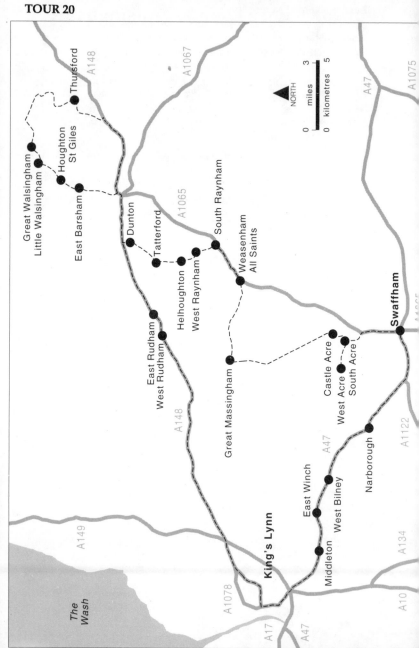

Tour 20 - King's Lynn to Walsingham

Leave King's Lynn heading south-east on the A47 and pass through Middleton, East Winch, West Bilney and Narborough, then turn left at the crossroads with the A1065. Take the next turn left through picturesque and historic countryside.

South Acre

The *Church of St George* has some fine brasses dating from 1384.

Head west on a well maintained country road.

West Acre

An Augustinian priory was founded here in 1100. The *Church of All Saints* is mainly 13th century.

Again on country roads, this time head east for Castle Acre which is visible for miles around.

Castle Acre

The ruins of a *Norman Castle* and the 13th century Bailey gate are worth exploring.

Set in farmland bordering the river Nar are the extensive and well cared for remains of a *Cluniac Priory* that was founded in the 11th century. The great west front of the church is a wonderful example of elaborate 12th century architecture. The prior's lodgings has a fine bay window and some of the rooms are still intact and contain interesting relics. The flint and brick gatehouse is worth seeing as is the walled herb garden.

The 13th century *Church of St James the Great* is outside the town's walls and was supposedly built on the site of an earlier Saxon building. The font and its cover, paintings and 15th century hexagonal pulpit are worth a visit.

Other places worth visiting are the centre of the village, the Norman town and Stocks Green, most of which date back to the 15th century.

Country Walks: There are many delightful walks in an around this pretty village where the ancient Peddars Way crosses the river Nar.

Leave Castle Acre on either of the two country roads heading north to the B1145. One road leads to Rougham, and from there turn left onto the B1145, then take the second road right for Great Massingham. The other road from Castle Acre crosses the B1145 for Great Massingham. Either way you will pass through very scenic countryside.

Great Massingham

A very attractive little village which boasts ponds at each end of the village green and another pond on the side road to Weasenham. The *Church of St Mary's* has a very tall tower which can be seen from miles around.

Leave on the country road heading east for Weasenham All Saints. After passing through this lovely little village turn left onto the A1065. Turn left in the village at South Raynham, and drive along country lanes, through glorious farmland to Helhoughton, still heading north to Tatterford. Turn right in the village and head north for Dunton beside the A148. Turn right onto the A148, then take the second major road to the left, the B1105.

East Barsham

The Tudor manor built by Sir Henry Fermor in 1520 to 1530, has a superb two-storeyed gatehouse, magnificent group of ten chimneys and windows that make this a wonderful example of early Tudor architecture.
All Saints' Church has a Norman south door and two pieces of very interesting sculpture dating from 1640.

Houghton St Giles

The main sight in this town is the Roman Catholic *National Shrine of Our Lady* with its small 14th century chapel.

Little Walsingham

A Medieval village with buildings that have beams jutting out over the pavement, although some have been sawn off. The High Street is full of charming and fascinating old buildings, the shops are interesting and *The Pump* is a famous landmark dating back to 1530.
The *Church of St Mary* is Perpendicular and was restored in 1961. The font is one of the finest in the county and stands on three steps, the top one being in the shape of a Maltese cross which is unusual.
Town trails: Walk around the ancient town and see the historic buildings. One mile out of town is the Shrine of Our Lady of Walsingham.

Great Walsingham

Information Centre: Shirehall Museum, Common Place, ph (01328) 820 510, open summer only.

Places to See

In the grounds of *Walsingham Abbey* is the famous site of the original shrine to Our Lady of Walsingham. The Abbey is the remains of an Augustinian priory.

Shirehall Museum, Common Place, ph (01328) 820 510, is open Easter to September daily 10am to 5pm and Sunday 2 to 5pm. Closed Monday 1pm to 2pm. October open Saturday and Sunday only.

Experience the harshness of past justice with a visit to the Georgian courtroom complete with truncheons, handcuffs and prisoners' cell.

Wells and Walsingham Railway is open daily from Easter to end September.

The Light Railway is the longest 10¼ inch narrow gauge steam railway in the world. The train ride offers a great day out in the countryside, stopping at the harbour town of Wells, the picturesque town of Walsingham and passing over five bridges. The train stops along the way and the journey time is approximately 30 minutes in each direction.

Cross the ford over the *River Stiffkey* and there is a tiny green, a memorial oak, a monument to Sir Eustace Gurney, and Berry Hall a manor house dating from 1520 complete with moat.

South of the village are the ruins of a very old church lying in a field near the 14th century *Church of St Peter*, which is on a slope overlooking the beautiful valley. It has fine window carvings and the original clerestory windows are still intact, one of the few examples to be found in the country. The bells date from 1330 and the beams are original from when the church was thatched.

Country Walks: Take a pleasant walk down the path past the church to the 13th century scratch dial, down the hill across the ford and up to the Hindringham Road where there is one of the best knapped-flint walls anywhere on the once Methodist now Russian Orthodox church.

Leave Great Walsingham on the B1388 heading north-east and take the third road on the right for Lower Green (which is well signposted). Head south through the countryside to Thursford beside the A148.

Thursford

The *Thursford Collection*, ph (01328) 878 477, is open daily from 1pm to 5pm in April, May, September and October, and from 11am to 5pm in June, July and August.

This is a sight and sound spectacular with live musical shows featuring a unique collection of mechanical organs and the wurlitzer show. Venetian gondola fairground rides, narrow gauge railway and the world's greatest collection of steam road engines are further attractions.

Leave Thursford by turning right onto the A148, passing through East Rudham, West Rudham and Hillington before returning to King's Lynn.

ACCOMMODATION INDEX
Self Catering

Brisley - Tour 9

Church Farm Cottages
Brisley
Dereham NR20 5LL
ph: (01362) 668 332
Contact: Mrs G Howes
2 cottages, sleep 2-5, open all year.
Weekly rate: £180.00-400.00.

Brick and flint 16th century cottages overlooking peaceful and tranquil village green. Children are welcome in these well-equipped cottages that have television, video, microwave, log fires and electric blankets. There is horse riding nearby.

Hindringham - Tour 12

Moat House & Banes Cottage
Hindringham Hall
Hindringham
Fakenham NR21 OQA
ph: (01328) 878 226
Contact: Mrs C Tucker
2 cottages both with 2 bedrooms (1 double & 2 single beds).
Weekly rate: from £200.00-410.00.

The cottages are within the grounds of a moated house set in 9 acres of delightful and peaceful gardens. Coin operated telephones (which take incoming calls), dishwasher, linen is provided, laundry facilities, central heating and electricity is by meter reading. Ideal base for touring many places of interest, and golf

is available nearby.

Little Walsingham - Tour 20

Back Lane Cottage
Back Lane
Little Walsingham
Contact: Mrs J Heal
Burgh Parva Hall
Melton Constable NR24 2PU
ph: (01263) 860 797
1 House, sleeps 5, open all year
Weekly rate: £160.00-365.00.

Charming cottage dating back to 1642 with lovely secluded garden in a pretty little village. Children are welcome, linen is provided and gas/electricity is by meter. Horse riding nearby.

Chantry Barn
Little Walsingham
Contact Mrs J Heal
Burgh Parva Hall
Melton Constable
ph: (01263) 860 797
1 house, sleeps 5-6, open all year
Weekly rate: £170.00-410.00.

Ancient barn has been carefully restored and discreetly designed with excellent facilities for the disabled. Children are welcome, linen is provided and gas/electricity is by meter. Horse riding and many places of interest make this lovely base set in a walled garden ideal for touring Norfolk.

Ludham - Tour 3

Corner & Crown Cottage
Contact: Ms Sparrow
Crown House
Ludham
Great Yarmouth NR29 5QE
2 Cottages, sleep 4-6, open all year
Weekly rate: £110.00-225.00.

Beautiful thatched cottages in the centre of a delightful village. Lovely exposed beams and linen is provided. Ideally situated for the coast, walking and touring.

North Walsham - Tour 6

Bradfield Hall Cottage
North Walsham NR28 0QW
ph: (01263) 833 200
1 cottage, sleeps 6-7, open all year
Weekly rate: £70.00-250.00

Well-equipped cottage set on a working dairy farm in the grounds of Bradfield Hall. Ideal base for the Broads, coast and many historic homes. Fishing, golf and horse riding are available nearby.

Salle - Tour 2

Coachman's Cottage
Salle Reepham
Contact: Mrs Sally Marshall
Salle Place
Salle
Reepham NR10 5SF
ph: (01603) 870 638
1 cottage, sleeps 4, open all year
Weekly rate: £95.00-200.00

Absolutely delightful typical Norfolk coachman's cottage in magnificent Old Rectory grounds with orchard, wood, lawns, half moat, stream and gardens. This has to be one of the most beautiful touring bases in Norfolk, where the accommodation is of a high standard and tastefully furnished. Sally and Geoff Marshall are the perfect "English Squire and Lady". Everyone is given an extremely warm welcome and children can feed the ducks that come to the back door every morning. The lounge has a wood burning stove (plenty of wood), the rest of the house centrally heated, electricity is by meter and linen is provided. Ample car parking available.

Snettisham - Tour 15

Cobb Cottage
Snettisham
Contact: Mr S Pink
Snettisham House
Snettisham
King's Lynn PE31 7RZ
1 cottage, sleeps 5, open all year
Weekly rate: £200.00-380.00.

Beautiful 18th century cottage set in its own secluded walled garden. Children are welcome and linen is provided. This is a non-smoking cottage.

Fisherman's & Curson's Cottages
Contact: Mrs A Campbell
Craven House
Lynn Road
Snettisham
King's Lynn PE31 7LW
2 cottages, sleep 4-5, open all year
Weekly rate: £140.00-275.00.

Attractive and comfortable stone cottages set in a lovely coastal village. Children are welcome and the cottages are well equipped and linen is provided. Boating, sailing, golf and horse riding are all within easy reach.

Bed & Breakfast

Aylsham - Tour 2

The Old Bank House
3 Norwich Road
Aylsham NR11 6BN
ph: (01263) 733 843
Contact: Enid Surridge
1 double, 1 twin, 1 family, 1 with ensuite, 2 private bathrooms
Single B&B: £17.20, Double B&B: £34.00.

A warm welcome awaits in this elegant Georgian house, formerly a private bank. Accommodation offers four-poster beds and olde worlde character, Victorian bathrooms and panelled rooms. Children are welcome, there is a games room and ample parking.

Barnham - Tour 11

Rymer Farm
Barnham
Thetford IP24 2PP
ph: (01842) 890 233
1 double, 1 twin, 1 single, 2 with ensuites 1 private bathroom.
Single B&B: £20.00, Double B&B: £32.00-36.00.

This 17th century farmhouse has a lovely lounge with a log fire in winter, and the hearty breakfasts are a great way to start the day. Ideally located for touring Norfolk and many historic places of interest, including Iceni Village and Grimes Graves. Children are welcome in this friendly home with its garden room and fishing pond.

Bracon Ash - Tour 10

The Old Bakery
The Street
Bracon Ash
Norwich NR14 8EL
ph: (01508) 570 360
1 double, 1 twin, 1 family, all with ensuites.
Single B&B: £18.00, Double B&B: £32.00

Former village bakery dating from 1725 set in a village only 5 miles from Norwich. Children are welcome and hearty farmhouse breakfasts are served. The gardens are lovely and horse riding, golf and fishing are available nearby.

Cawston - Tour 2

The Walnuts
8/12 New Street
Cawston
Norwich NR10 4AL
ph: (01603) 871 357
1 single, 2 double, 1 with private facilities, 1 public bathroom.
Single B&B: from £20.00, Double B&B: from £34.00

Delightful cottage set in an acre of lovely gardens with a swimming pool, only 9 miles from Norwich. Television, radio/alarm clocks and tea/coffee making facilities in all the rooms and there is a pay phone in the hall. Good local pubs, restaurants, golf and horse riding are available nearby. Children over 6 are welcome to this charming home, where special rates apply for winter and short breaks.

Coltishall - Tour 4

The Norfolk Mead Hotel
Coltishall NR12 7DN
ph: (01603) 737 521
8 double/twin, 2 family all with private facilities or ensuites.
Single B&B: from £49.00, Double B&B: from £65.00.

Charming Georgian manor house set in 12 riverside acres of Norfolk Broads. A warm welcome and happy atmosphere along with a fine restaurant, bar and lounge with log fires in winter. There is an outdoor swimming pool, rowing, fishing, horse riding and bird-watching available for the use of guests.

Cromer - Tour 5

The Grove
95 Overstrand Road
Cromer NR27 0DJ
ph: (01263) 512 412
2 single, 3 double, 3 twin, 2 family, 7 with ensuites, 2 private bathrooms.
Single B&B: £17.50-21.00, Double B&B: £35.00-42.00.

Georgian home set in 3 acres with beautiful walks through fields and woods to the cliffs and beach. This peaceful home, where children are welcome, is set in a quiet location only ½ mile from the town centre. There are also self catering cottages in the grounds. Golf, horse riding, fishing and bird watching are all available nearby.

Great Yarmouth - Tour 3

Spindrift Private Hotel
36 Wellesley Road
Great Yarmouth NR30 1EU
ph: (01493) 858 674
2 single, 2 double, 1 twin, 2 family, 5 with ensuites, 1 private bathroom.
Single B&B: £16.00, Double B&B: £26.40.

Small private hotel where the front bedrooms have excellent sea views and children are welcome. One of Britain's major seaside resorts with 5 miles of seafront and an award-winning leisure complex, busy harbour and fishing centre.

Grimston - Tour 14

Congham Hall
Grimston
King's Lynn PE32 1AH
ph: (01485) 600 250
1 single, 4 double, 9 twin, all with ensuites
Single B&B: from £75.00, Double B&B: from £99.00.

Fantastic Georgian manor country house set in beautiful gardens and parkland. A warm welcome awaits all guests and children over 12 years in this delightfully furnished home, with some rooms having four poster beds. Special rates apply for winter and short breaks. Golf, horse riding, outdoor swimming pool, tennis and bird watching are just some of the extras, making this an ideal touring base or a great place to just relax.

Happisburgh - Tour 6

The Hill House
Happisburgh
ph: (01692) 650 004
Self contained double, ensuite
B&B: £30.00 (£20.00 single)

Lovely Tudor pub next to the church. Sir Arthur Conan Doyle wrote *The Dancing Men* in a room with a window overlooking the beautiful golden sands. The self-contained double room was built as a Victorian signal box, but there never has been a railway here. This is a very popular pub, with excellent meals, very attractive beer garden, and children are welcome.

Heydon - Tour 2

Cropton Hall
Heydon
Saxthorpe NR11 6RX
Contact: Mrs K Easy
Single B&B: £15.00-22.50, Double B&B: £29.00-45.00.

Small Jacobean country hall set in 3 acres of rural conservation area. Wonderful home cooked meals, log fires, and a warm welcome await

guests, children and pets (by arrangement) in this charming house. All rooms have ensuites, television and tea making facilities. Covered swimming pool (in season), jacuzzi and billiard table. Horse riding, golf, country walks and bird watching are all nearby.

Hunstanton - Tour 16

Wash & Tope Hotel
Le Strange Terrace
Hunstanton PE36 5AJ
ph: (01485) 532 250
4 double, 4 twin, 2 family, 6 with ensuites 3 private bathrooms.
Single B&B: from £15.00, Double B&B from £30.00.

Traditional inn with two bars and two restaurants, where children are welcome. Great sea views, four posters beds and television in the rooms make this a lovely way to spend time at the seaside. Fishing, golf and bird watching are nearby.

King's Lynn - Tour 16

Tudor Rose Hotel
St Nicholas Street
King's Lynn PE30 1LR
ph: (01553) 762 824
Contact: John and Andrea Bull
6 double, 3 twin, 5 single, all with ensuites
Single B&B: £38.50, Double B&B: £50.00.

Beautiful 15th century timbered hotel in the town centre where children are welcome, and excellent service and lovely meals await.

Special rates apply for winter and short breaks. Fishing and golf are available nearby.

Melton Constable - Tour 2

Burgh Parva Hall
Melton
Constable NR24 2PU
ph: (01263) 860 797
1 double, 1 twin, sharing 1 bathroom.
Single B&B: from £16.00.

Attractive 16th century farmhouse in lovely rural position within easy walking to Melton Constable, and ideally situated for the coast and the many attractions and historic homes in the area. Tea/coffee making facilities in the rooms and an iron is available.

Mundford - Tour 17

Colveston Manor
Mundford
Thetford IP26 5HU
ph: (01842) 878 218
2 double, 1 twin, some with private facilities
Single B&B: from £17.00, Double B&B: from £34.00.

Spacious comfortable non-smoking farmhouse with a lovely garden in a rural setting in the heart of Breckland. Children are welcome, and some rooms have four-poster beds. Hearty farmhouse breakfasts and lovely dinners make this an ideal base for visiting many places of interest. Horse riding, golf, country walks and fishing are some of the added attractions.

Neatishead - Tour 4

Barton Angler Country Inn
Irstead Road
Neatishead
Wroxham NR12 8XP
ph: (01692) 630 740
3 single, 4 double, 5 private bathrooms.
Single B&B: £20.00, Double B&B £56.00.
Reductions for 2 night and 7 night stays.

Previously an early Regency rectory, now a country inn with a 4 acre garden adjacent to lovely Barton Broad. Fishing, golf and boats for hire, and there is horse riding nearby. Some rooms have four-poster beds, and the delicious evening meals make this an ideal touring base.

North Elmham - Tour 9

Millers Old Cottage
High Street
North Elmham
Dereham NR20 5JX
ph: (01362) 668 813
1 single, 2 double/twin 1 with ensuite and 1 public bathroom.
Single B&B: from £14.00, Double B&B: from £28.00.

Large comfortable 17th century beamed cottage with inglenook fireplaces, in historic Saxon village and close to cathedral ruins. Television, tea/coffee making facilities in all rooms.

Norwich - Tour 2

Barnham Broom Hotel, Golf, Conference & Leisure Complex

Barnham Broom
Norwich NR9 4DD
ph: (01603) 759 393
52 rooms all with ensuites.
Single B&B: from £59.50, Double
B&B: from £82.00.

This hotel is set in a beautiful valley, and children are welcome. The complex offers a wide range of activities including two 18 hole golf courses, 4 squash courts, 3 tennis courts, heated indoor pool, gym, sauna and solarium. The two bars, lovely spacious lounge and ground floor rooms are accessible for wheelchairs. There is also a hairdressing salon. Special rates apply for short breaks. All rooms have tea/coffee making facilities, telephones and televisions. Places of interest nearby include Blickling Hall, Felbrigg Hall, Grimes Graves, Holkham Hall, Norfolk Broads, Coast and Norwich.

Pulham Market - Tour 8

The Old Bakery
Church Walk
Pulham Market
Diss IP21 4SJ
ph: (01379) 676 492
2 twin, 1 family, all with ensuites.
Single B&B: £28.00-32.00, Double
B&B: £36.00-44.00

Oak framed house with spiral staircase dating from 1580 set in a delightful village. Children are welcome at this non-smoking home where traditional cooking is carried out by a master chef. Relax in friendly comfort in tastefully

furnished rooms with television and tea/coffee making facilities. Horse riding and golf are available nearby.

Rollesby - Tour 3

The Old Court House
Court Road
Rollesby
Great Yarmouth NR29 5HG
ph: (01493) 369 665
Contact: Ben and Anthea Marrimer
2 double, 1 twin, 4 family, 5 with ensuites, 2 private bathrooms.
Double B&B: from £38.00.

Peaceful, quiet country hotel set in 4 acres of lovely grounds with heated outdoor pool. Children are welcome in this family run hotel where home cooking is excellent. Bicycles for hire, fishing, tennis, horse riding, boating and beaches nearby make this a very attractive place to spend time. There is an 18 hole golf course at Caister. Special rates apply for short breaks.

Wells-next-the-Sea - Tour 12

Scarborough House Hotel
Clubbs Lane
Wells-next-the-Sea NR23 1DP
ph: 01328 710309
10 double, 3 twin, 1 family, all with ensuites
Single B&B: £29.00-34.00, Double
B&B £48.00-58.00.

Luxury hotel with four poster beds, beamed restaurant and lovely bar. Children and dogs are welcome and ground floor accommodation is available. This is an ideal place for bird watching and walking, and golf and fishing are available nearby. Special rates apply from October to April.

Winterton-on-Sea - Tour 4

Tower Cottage
Black Street
Winterton-on-Sea NR29 4AP
ph: (01493) 394 053
Contact: Mrs M Webster
1 double with ensuite, & sitting room in converted barn overlooking the cottage garden.
1 double, 1 twin.
Single B&B: £14.00.

18th century flint cottage still has many original features and overlooks the pretty village church. This charming home where children over 5 are welcome, serves a very generous and hearty breakfast with homemade bread and preserves. Ideal touring base for the Broads, Norwich and the coast, and is only a few minutes from a lovely sandy beach.

The Fisherman's Return
Winterton-on-Sea
ph: (01493) 393 305
3 double, 1 single.
From £20.00 per person.

Converted 300-year-old fishermen's cottages. Photographs and landscapes adorn the walls of this charming pub with an open fire in the winter. The rooms are charming with sloping ceilings and tea/coffee making facilities. The beach and coastline are exhilarating. Meals are excellent and are home-cooked, recommended by several leading accommodation guides.

Wolferton - Tour 12

The Old Rectory
Wolferton
Sandringham PE31 6HF
ph: 01485 540496
1 double, 2 twin, 2 with ensuite and 1 private bathroom
Single B&B: £35.00, Double B&B: £55.00-60.00.

Quiet country house set in 4½ acres of wooded grounds within the Sandringham estate. Children are welcome in this warm and friendly 19th century Norfolk carrstone hotel, a winner of the 1993 Excellence Award. Ideal for walks, bird watching, 18 hole golf course at Hunstanton and tennis.

Wroxham - Tour 4

The Mount
93 Norwich Road
Wroxham NR12 8RX
ph: (01603) 783 909
3 double/twin, 2 with private facilities, 1 public bathroom.
Single B&B: from £20.00, Double B&B: from £32.00.

Delightful Georgian cottage at the heart of the Broads. Secluded car parking enables guests to leave their car while enjoying the activities the Broads offer. Fishing, golf and boat cruises are all available nearby.

INDEX OF SIGHTS AND ATTRACTIONS

| Thetford | Castle Hill earthworks | Tour 11 |
| Weeting | remains | Tour 17 |

Churches and Chapels

Houghton St Giles	Slipper Chapel	Tour 20
Little Barningham	St Andrew's church	Tour 5
Salle	St Peter & St Paul	Tour 2
Thetford	Church of the Holy Sepulchre	Tour 11

Early Closing Days

Attleborough	Wednesday	Tour 10
Aylsham	Wednesday	Tour 2
Caister-on-Sea	Wednesday	Tour 3
Cromer	Wednesday	Tour 5
Diss	Tuesday	Tour 10
Downham Market	Wednesday	Tour 18
Fakenham	Wednesday	Tour 9
Gressenhall	Wednesday	Tour 9
Hingham	Wednesday	Tour 13
Hunstanton	Thursday	Tour 16
King's Lynn	Wednesday	Tour 14
Loddon	Wednesday	Tour 7
Ludham	Wednesday	Tour 4
North Walsham	Wednesday	Tour 6
Sheringham	Thursday	Tour 5
Stalham	Wednesday	Tour 4
Swaffham	Thursday	Tour 18
Watton	Thursday	Tour 11
Wells-next-the-Sea	Thursday	Tour 12
Wroxham	Wednesday	Tour 4
Wymondham	Wednesday	Tour 11

Farm Parks

Caister-on-Sea	Thrigby Hall Wildlife Gardens	Tour 3
Fakenham	Pensthorpe Wildfowl Park	Tour 9
Fakenham	Mill Farm Rare Breeds-Hindringham	Tour 9
Great Yarmouth	Norfolk Rare Breeds	Tour 3
Great Yarmouth	Butterfly Farm	Tour 3
Gressenhall	Union Farm	Tour 9
Hindringham	Mill Farm Rare Breeds	Tour 12
Hoveton	Wroxham Barns & Junior Farm	Tour 4
Reedham	Pettitt's Animal Adventure Park	Tour 7
Snettisham	Park Farm	Tour 15
West Runton	Norfolk Shire Horse Centre	Tour 5

Gardens & Parks

Aylsham	Mannington Hall	Tour 2
Aylsham	Wolterton Park	Tour 2
Bressingham	Bressingham Hall Gardens	Tour 10
Caister-on-Sea	Thrigby Hall	Tour 3
Felbrigg	Felbrigg Hall Gardens	Tour 5
Gooderstone	Water Gardens	Tour 13
Heacham	Caley Mill Herb Garden	Tour 15
Holkham	Holkham Hall Gardens	Tour 19
Hoveton	Hall Gardens	Tour 4
North Walsham	Rose Garden Centre	Tour 6
Norwich	Fairhaven Gardens	Tour 1
Oxborough	Oxburgh Hall Gardens	Tour 13
Raveningham	Raveningham Hall gardens	Tour 7
Sandringham	Gardens & Grounds	Tour 15
Sheringham	Park & Gardens	Tour 5
Swanington	Manor gardens	Tour 2

Guildhalls

Blakeney		Tour 12
Great Yarmouth	Town Hall	Tour 3
King's Lynn	Holy Trinity	Tour 14
King's Lynn	St George's	Tour 14
Norwich		Tour 1

Houses - open to the public

Aylsham	Wolterton Park	Tour 2
Blickling	Blickling Hall	Tour 2
Bressingham	Bressingham Hall	Tour 10
Felbrigg	Felbrigg Hall	Tour 5
Holkham	Holkham Hall	Tour 19
King's Lynn	Houghton Hall	Tour 14
Oxborough	Oxburgh Hall	Tour 13
Sandringham	Sandringham House	Tour 15
Sheringham	Beeston Hall	Tour 5

Historic Sites

Brandon	Grimes Graves	Tour 17
Caister-on-Sea	Caister Roman Site	Tour 3
Cockley Cley	Iceni Village	Tour 17
North Elmham	Saxon earthworks	Tour 9
Thetford	Redcastle Norman earthworks	Tour 11

Hospitals

Cromer	Mill Road	Tour 5

Great Yarmouth	Northgate St	Tour 3
Great Yarmouth	Queens Rd	Tour 3
King's Lynn	London Rd	Tour 14
Norwich	St Stephen's Rd	Tour 1
Wisbech	The Park	Tour 18

Hotels and Pubs

Ingham	The Swan Inn	Tour 4
Swanton Morley	Angel Inn	Tour 9

Information Centres

Great Yarmouth	Town Hall	Tour 3
Hunstanton	The Green	Tour 16
King's Lynn	The Old Gaol House	Tour 14
Norwich	Guildhall	Tour 1
Sheringham	Station Approach	Tour 5
Wisbech	Library, Ely Place	Tour 18
Wymondham	Middleton St	Tour 11

Leisure Centres

Fritton	Fritton Lake	Tour 7

Market Days

Acle	Thursday	Tour 3
Attleborough	Thursday	Tour 10
Aylsham	Monday & Tuesday	Tour 2
Brandon	Thursday & Saturday	Tour 17
Cromer	Friday	Tour 5
Diss	Friday	Tour 10
Downham Market	Friday	Tour 18
Fakenham	Thursday	Tour 9
Great Yarmouth	Wednesday, Friday & Saturday	Tour 3
Gressenhall	Tuesday & Friday	Tour 9
Hunstanton	Wednesday & Sunday	Tour 16
King's Lynn	Tuesday, Friday & Saturday	Tour 14
North Walsham	Thursday	Tour 6
Norwich	Monday to Saturday	Tour 1
Reepham	Wednesday	Tour 9
Sheringham	Saturday	Tour 5
Stalham	Tuesday	Tour 4
Swaffham	Saturday	Tour 18
Watton	Wednesday	Tour 11
Wells-next-the-Sea	Wednesday	Tour 12
Wymondham	Friday	Tour 11

Snettisham	Bird Reserve	Tour 15
Titchwell	Bird Reserve	Tour 16

Police Stations

Cromer	Holt Rd	Tour 5
Great Yarmouth	Howard St North	Tour 3
Hunstanton	King's Lynn Rd	Tour 16
King's Lynn	St James Rd	Tour 14
Norwich	Bethel St	Tour 1
Sheringham	Weybourne Rd	Tour 5
Swaffham	Westacre Rd	Tour 18
Thetford	Norwich Rd	Tour 11
Wisbech	Lynn Rd	Tour 18
Wymondham	Avenue Rd	Tour 11

Railways

Aylsham	Bure Valley	Tour 2
Great Walsingham	Wells & Walsingham	Tour 20
Sheringham	North Norfolk	Tour 5
Wolferton	Station Museum	Tour 15
Wroxham	Bure Valley	Tour 4
Wroxham	Barton House Railway	Tour 4
Wymondham	Railway Station Buffet	Tour 11

Vineyards

East Dereham	Elmham Park	Tour 11
East Harling	Harling	Tour 11
North Elmham	Elmham Park	Tour 9
Pulham Market	Pulham Vineyards	Tour 8
Thelnathan	Thelnathan	Tour 11

Walks

Blickling	Blickling Hall	Tour 2
Blickling	Weavers Way	Tour 2
Brancaster	Scolt Head Island	Tour 16
Brandon	Brandon Country Park	Tour 17
Brandon	Santon Downham	Tour 17
Brandon	Thetford Forest	Tour 17
Castle Acre	Country walk	Tour 20
Coltishall	Country walk	Tour 4
Cromer	Weavers Way	Tour 5
Cromer	Town trails	Tour 5
Felbrigg	Felbrigg Hall	Tour 5
Great Walsingham	Country walks	Tour 20
Great Yarmouth	Weavers Way	Tour 3

Zoo

Banham		Tour 10

Other Places of Interest

Brandon	Thetford Forest	Tour 17
Brandon	Heritage Centre	Tour 17
Brandon	Brandon Country Park	Tour 17
Castle Acre	Earthworks	Tour 20
Castle Rising	Trinity Hospital	Tour 15
Cromer	Beacon Hill	Tour 5
Great Yarmouth	Nelson's Monument	Tour 3
Great Yarmouth	Town wall	Tour 3
Great Yarmouth	Brass Rubbing Centre	Tour 3
Great Yarmouth	Old Merchant's House	Tour 3
Great Yarmouth	Lydia Eva Steam Drifter	Tour 3
Grimes Graves	Flint Mines	Tour 17
Heacham	Lavender Distillery	Tour 15
Hunstanton	Heacham Lavender Distillery	Tour 16
King's Lynn	Hampton Court	Tour 14
King's Lynn	Old Gaol House	Tour 14
King's Lynn	Clifton House	Tour 14
King's Lynn	Caithness Crystal	Tour 14
Langham	Crystal	Tour 12
Norwich	Brass Rubbing Centre	Tour 1
Paston	Barn	Tour 6
Reedham	Taxidermist	Tour 7
Sheringham	Peter's Bookshop	Tour 5
Swaffham	Market Cross	Tour 18
Thetford	King's House	Tour 11
Thursford	Mechanical Collection	Tour 20
Wisbech	Peckover House	Tour 18
Wolferton	Railway Station	Tour 15
Wymondham	Market Cross	Tour 11

Craft Centres

Cley next the Sea	Made in Cley	Tour 12
Erpingham	Alby Lace & Crafts	Tour 5
Great Yarmouth	Great Yarmouth Pottery	Tour 3
Great Yarmouth	Candlemaker & Model Centre	Tour 3
Holkham	Pottery	Tour 19
Holt	The Old Workshop	Tour 5
Hoveton	Wroxham Barns & Junior Farm	Tour 4
King's Lynn	Caithness Crystal	Tour 14
Langham	Hand made Crystal	Tour 12
Loddon	Loddon Water Mill Crafts	Tour 7

Golf

Attleborough	Barnham Broom Complex	Tour 10
Cley next the Sea	Sheringham Golf Club	Tour 12
Cley next the Sea	Royal Cromer Golf Club	Tour 12
Costessey	Costessey Golf Club	Tour 1
Cromer	Royal Cromer Golf Club	Tour 5
Diss	Diss Golf Club	Tour 10
Downham Market	Ryston Park - Denver	Tour 18
East Dereham	Dereham Golf Club	Tour 11
East Dereham	Reymerston Golf Club	Tour 11
Fakenham	Fakenham Golf Club	Tour 9
Fritton	Fritton Lake	Tour 7
Fritton	Caldecott Hall Golf Club	Tour 7
Great Yarmouth	Caldecott Hall Golf Club	Tour 3
Hunstanton	Hunstanton Golf Club	Tour 16
King's Lynn	King's Lynn Golf Club	Tour 14
Mundesley	Mundesley Golf Club	Tour 6
Norwich	Barnham Broom Complex	Tour 1
Norwich	Eaton Golf Club	Tour 1
Norwich	Royal Norwich	Tour 1
Sheringham	Sheringham Golf Club	Tour 5
Shipdham	Swaffham Golf Club	Tour 11
Sprowston	Sprowston Golf Course	Tour 4
Swaffham	Swaffham Golf Club	Tour 18
Taverham	Wensum Valley Golf Club	Tour 9
Thetford	Thetford Golf Club	Tour 11
Watton	Watton Golf Club	Tour 11
West Runton	Links Country Park Golf Club	Tour 5
Wymondham	Barnham Broom Complex	Tour 11

Horse Riding

Aylsham	Four Horseshoes	Tour 2
Caister-on-Sea	Caister Riding School	Tour 3
Cawston	Albion Ride	Tour 2
Fritton	Caldecott Hall	Tour 7
Hockwold	Hockwold Lodge	Tour 17
Mundesley	Bridge Farm Stables - Gimingham	Tour 6
Pulham St Mary	Waveney Valley	Tour 8
South Lopham	Rosebrook Equestrian	Tour 10
West Runton	West Runton Riding	Tour 5
West Runton	Norfolk Shire Horse Centre	Tour 5

Tennis Courts

Blakeney	Blakeney Tennis	Tour 12

INDEX OF TOWNS

OTHER TITLES BY LITTLE HILLS PRESS

DRIVING GUIDES

Australia's Central & Western Outback	A$24.95
Australia's Northern Outback	A$24.95
Australia's Eastern Outback	A$24.95
Driving Guide to Britain - Norfolk	A$11.95
Driving Guide to Britain - Suffolk	A$11.95

LITTLE HILLS GUIDES

Australia	A$19.95
Australia's Great Barrier Reef	A$14.95
Bali	A$11.95
California	A$11.95
Cambodia	A$14.95
Cuba	A$16.95
Europe	A$14.95
Hawaii	A$11.95
Hong Kong & Macau	A$16.95
India	A$ 9.95
Korea (nyp)	A$14.95
New Zealand	A$16.95
Outback Australia	A$19.95
Singapore & Malaysia	A$14.95
Tasmania	A$14.95
Thailand	A$11.95

POCKET GUIDE BOOKS

Brisbane & Gold Coast (nyp)	A$ 9.95
London	A$ 5.95
Moscow (nyp)	A$ 9.95
Perth & Margaret River (nyp)	A$ 9.95
Singapore	A$ 5.95
Sydney (nyp)	A$ 9.95

FOR ORDERS & ENQUIRIES CONTACT:-

LITTLE HILLS PRESS
11/37-43 Alexander Street, Crows Nest. NSW 2065
Fax: (612) 9438-5762 Tel: (612) 9437-6995
Email: littlehills@peg.apc.org
Home Page: http://www.peg.apc.org/~littlehills